All the Presidents' Gardens

The East Garden, designed during the Wilson administration by Beatrix Farrand,
in a 1921 photograph by Frances Benjamin Johnston.

All the Presidents' Gardens

∽

Madison's Cabbages to Kennedy's Roses—
How the White House Grounds
Have Grown with America

Marta McDowell

TIMBER PRESS
PORTLAND, OREGON

This 1899 cover of the Iowa Seed Company catalog featured the White House, 'Old Glory' geraniums, and elaborate pattern bedding, as well as the forty-five-star flag that flew from 1896 to 1907.

Contents

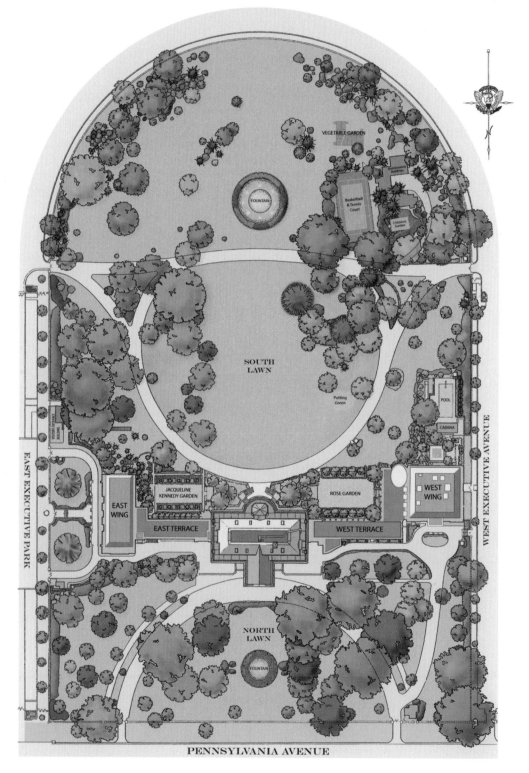

The White House grounds.

Preface

THE UNITED STATES was too big. For a topic, that is. When my editor suggested I might write a history of American gardening, I sat at my desk. Stunned. It seemed a subject broad as a sea of grass, long and muddy as the Mississippi, elusive as a white whale that would, after a mad, obsessed chase, drag me under.

Regional differences are vast. What grows happily for friends in Denver sulks, then dies, in my humid New Jersey garden. Then there are questions of influence that vary across the wide waist of the continent: the Spanish with their patio and courtyard gardens from Florida to California, the tidy colonial gardens of New England, the immense plantations of the antebellum South. And with more than five-plus centuries, depending on how you count, the players involved in American horticulture and landscape design are legion.

Two people convinced me to take on this quest—one dead, one alive. The reason I study, teach, and write about garden history is because of Beatrix Jones Farrand (1872–1959). On my first visit to the grounds of Dumbarton Oaks in Georgetown in the 1980s, I was smitten with it and Farrand, its designer, one of the country's first landscape architects. It was about Beatrix Farrand that I taught my first class at the New York Botanical Garden.

Some years later one of my landscape history students, Seamus Maclennan, chose the White House grounds as the topic for his final project. It was

The lower 48.

riveting, a fifteen-minute chronicle of change in one of America's most recognizable landscapes. There were victory gardens and flowerbeds, glasshouses and putting greens, all set in the context of American history. For the problem now before me, it would set bounds, but also pull in a cast of characters and a VIP setting. Before I embarked on this undertaking Seamus graciously gave me leave to use his idea, proving once again, if you want to hum along with the Rodgers and Hammerstein tune, "that if you become a teacher, by your pupils you'll be taught."

Even with this approach, given the number of presidents plus first ladies, gardeners, architects, and the like, I've had to impose some economies in terms of scope. If, for example, Zachary Taylor is your favorite president, you will be disappointed. As neither he nor his wife were involved in the White House gardens, they do not appear in the narrative. "Summer White

Houses" were eliminated, though I was sorely tempted by places like Warm Springs, Georgia, Franklin Roosevelt's retreat south of Atlanta, and Rancho del Cielo, Reagan's Western White House. The fourteen White House head gardeners' biographies tell an interesting story in their own right so we see them together in "First Gardeners" at the back of the book.

I have defaulted to common names of plants in the body of the book. For those who prefer proper botanical nomenclature, you will find it in a back section, "All the Presidents' Plants"—a look at White House plantings over the past two centuries—and the index. If you had hoped for a complete list of plants named for presidents and first ladies, I did too. Unfortunately in most cases these cultivars have not stood the test of time, at least in terms of the marketplace. A rhododendron named 'Mrs. Grover Cleveland' might have been a big seller in the 1890s but soon disappeared from the nursery trade.

Long-term White House head gardener Irvin Williams once said, "What's great about the job is that our trees, our plants, our shrubs, know nothing about politics." Despite the presidential focus of the book, I have attempted to emulate the politics of plants. Because whether gardeners lean right or left, blue or red, we are united by a love of green growing things and the land in which they grow.

Fig. 22. ZEA MAIS RUBRA. MAÏS ROUGE.

Fig. 23. ZEA MAIS VERSICOLOR. MAÏS JASPÉ.

Fig. 24 ÉPI A GRAINS DE DIVERSES VARIÉTÉS.

The variety of corn raised by Native Americans and earlier settlers is still called Indian corn. From *Histoire naturelle, agricole et économique du maïs* by Matthieu Bonafous, 1836.

The Pursuit of Happiness

S INCE 1800, THE WHITE HOUSE has served as a residence for the president of the United States. The eighteen acres that surround the White House have been the Forrest Gump of gardens—an unwitting witness to history—a backdrop for Civil War soldiers, suffragettes, protestors in the 1960s, and activists today. Kings and queens have dined there. Bills and treaties have been signed. On its lawn presidents have landed and retreated. The front and back yard for the first family, it is by extension the nation's first garden.

The White House gardens mirror the country's horticultural aspirations over time. If "melting pot" has been a persistent metaphor for American culture, American horticulture shares the pedigree. The garden styles of the colonies, and later the United States, were borrowed from Europe and farther afield and then shaped by local traditions, by geography and climate, by transportation, economics, and innovation.

The White House that we know today was not in the mind of English explorer John Smith when he first sailed up the "Patawomeck" on a June day in 1608. When the wooden boat turned from the Chesapeake Bay into the mouth of the broad river, he and his fourteen-man crew were looking for the passage to the South Seas. Instead they found forests, fish, and farms. Along the Potomac that summer, they encountered native villages and with the villages, gardens bearing their summer abundance.

A 1667 map shows the future location of Washington D.C. at the confluence of the Potomac and the Anacostia—what the mapmaker called the Maryland—rivers.

John Smith met the tribal leader Powhatan who, in this detail of a 1612 map, is shown holding his pipe of tobacco.

"The Towne of Secota," from Thomas Hariot's 1588 book *A Briefe and True Report of the New Found Land of Virginia*, is similar to villages John Smith encountered on the Potomac in 1608.

Tobacco was a sensation in Europe, and so profitable for Virginia planters that early governors had to require some acreage be reserved for grain to avoid food shortages.

Corn was the main crop. Not the juicy sweet ears to which we have become accustomed, but Indian corn: hard kernels that had to be soaked or ground. It sustained life during the hungry season. Other food crops were also in evidence: beans, squash, sunflowers, and goosefoot (a relative of quinoa), and, for smoking rather than eating, tobacco. To his London Company John Smith wrote, "Heaven and earth never agreed better to frame a place for mans habitation . . . were it fully manured and inhabited by an industrious people."

Industrious settlers soon followed, pursuing not so much happiness as the right to plant and cash in on the brown gold that was tobacco. George Washington's ancestors were among those who emigrated from England and settled in the rich Virginia countryside below the Great Falls of the Potomac. The subjects of the Court of St. James, as well as the rest of Europe, presumed an unquestioned cultural superiority over the native people and a God-given right to "improve" this new land.

When the Potomac shoreline that John Smith had explored was finally chosen as the capital city of the brand-new United States of America, George Washington knew it needed a place for the president to call home. And that home would need a garden. This book is the story of that garden, and a story of gardening American-style.

Versailles
on the
Potomac

&

I am led to reflect how much more delightful to an undebauched mind is the task of
making improvements to the earth, than
all the vainglory which can be acquired
from ravaging it, by the most uninter-
rupted career of conquests.

GEORGE WASHINGTON in a letter to Arthur Young,
an English agricultural writer, 1788

THE 1790S

(1789–1797) GEORGE AND MARTHA WASHINGTON

ALL POLITICS IS local, as the saying goes, and so by necessity is gardening. George Washington selected a site for the nation's capital just fifteen miles upstream on the Potomac from his home at Mount Vernon, though on the opposite bank. He oversaw the plans for the new city, its buildings and green spaces, including the future White House. He was the first president, but he was creating his last garden.

The location of the White House and its surrounding federal city was by no means certain. In the early years of nationhood, Congress bounced from Philadelphia to Annapolis to Trenton to New York. There was even a brief move to Princeton, New Jersey, after a rabble of soldiers demanding back pay accosted Congress in the Pennsylvania Statehouse. The Constitution, ratified in May 1790, stipulated a "District (not exceeding ten Miles square) ... [as] the Seat of the Government of the United States." It did not specify its whereabouts. States and territories vied for the privilege the way countries bid for the Olympic Games today, and for the same reasons: money, power, prestige.

Washington and his fellow southerners, including Thomas Jefferson and James Madison, hoped for a Potomac site from the start. It was, they argued, the geographic center of the thirteen states. With plans under-way for canals to connect the river with the Great Lakes, the Potomac set a path to the west—the lure of land in the Ohio Valley already singing its

A view of Mount Vernon by an unknown artist showing the entry court, meandering paths, and some of Washington's collection of trees.

siren song. Northerners did not agree. Philadelphia, after all, was cosmopolitan in comparison with the relative backwaters of Maryland and Virginia. One Massachusetts journalist called the Potomac site "a Virginia delusion." The *New-York Journal* ran a black-edged mourning announcement: "To the memory of *Potowmacus*, who was the twin of *Philadelphia*—He was the child of Miss Assumption, a deluded female."

But the Potomac site turned out to be no misassumption, due to the political skills of its promoters. For perhaps the first time in the American epic, a dinner party changed history. The site of the capital was a bipartisan deal, brokered by a small pantheon of American gods in New York City. Thomas Jefferson hosted supper one night in 1790 at his Maiden Lane rental, lubricating the event "with punch and Madeira." James Madison and Alexander Hamilton made their way down the narrow streets of lower Manhattan to join him in the long twilight of a late June evening.

The three were colleagues, though hardly congenial. Tall, lean Jefferson, at the time the secretary of state, and the diminutive Madison, the Speaker of the House of Representatives, opposed Secretary of the Treasury Alexander Hamilton and his views on national control. But the dinner, or perhaps the Madeira, worked its magic. In exchange for throwing their support behind Hamilton's bill to have the federal government assume the states' war debts—Jefferson called this "a pill peculiarly bitter to the Southern States"—Hamilton went along with having the federal government reside on the Potomac. In early July the Residence Act squeaked through Congress, and on July 16, President Washington signed it into law. Philadelphia would act as temporary capital for the next decade, with the final move to a new ten-mile-square district targeted for the first Monday in December 1800. (In 1846, Congress gave one-third of the District back to Virginia, thus removing that portion of the original square southwest of the Potomac River.)

And so the future gardens at the White House were set on their trajectory. Congress provided George Washington broad powers to supervise the development of the as-yet-unnamed new city. As a war hero and unanimously elected president, he was riding a wave of popularity. Congress also gave him the privilege of choosing the exact location for the district within some seventy miles of Potomac riverfront. The tract of land that Washington selected was at an elbow of two rivers, the confluence of the Potomac and the Eastern Branch, or Anacostia.

The new capital and its gardens started, as with most garden projects, with a real estate transaction or, in this case, transactions. Maryland and Virginia ceded public lands while the city commissioners negotiated with private landowners, paying them per acre for their property. George Washington haggled with a few holdouts—speculators expecting a premium—including one he labeled "the obstinate Mr. Burns."

The George Washington who established Washington D.C. is easy to visualize, as the timing roughly coincides with the familiar Gilbert Stuart portrait that looks out at us from the dollar bill. Washington was physically imposing with prominent features and a legendary stiff upper lip. His hair had begun to recede from his forehead leaving his features in relief, as if waiting for Mount Rushmore. Hair powdered, posture erect, his six-foot frame was clad in a fashionable long coat made to his specifications. Famous as a man of few, select words, Washington once said, "With me it has always been a maxim rather to let my designs appear from my works than by my expressions."

At this point in the story, let us picture George Washington and his designs for Mount Vernon, his Virginia home, designs that would influence the gardens-to-come at the White House. The landscape at Mount Vernon occupied many hours of his time when the demands of government allowed. Stepping out from the pedimented doorway of his home, he could proceed right or left along a serpentine walk lined with weeping willows.

Like most serious gardeners, Washington was a bit plant-crazy. He asked friends and relations to send seeds and cuttings for his garden. Packets arrived from England, the Caribbean, and the Deep South. For his tender specimens—oranges and lemons, palms and palmettos—he built an expansive brick orangery, a building heated with stoves and lit with long south-facing windows. He planted so many roses that it took twelve days each June for the petals to be picked; his wife, Martha, distilled them into rosewater. He ordered plants in quantity from nurseries in Philadelphia and made a special trip to see William Prince's nursery, the large and grandly named Linnaean Botanic Garden, in Flushing, New York.

Washington liked to visit nurseries. Two generations of Bartrams—father John and sons John and William—collected plants, then propagated and sold them from a farm on the west bank of the Schuylkill River on the outskirts of Philadelphia. Some years earlier, during the 1787 Constitutional Convention, Washington had taken a jaunt to Bartram's farm, breakfasting with a friend then riding the three miles out from city center. The nursery's curious plants, many of which were exotic—that is, imported—were impressive, but the garden "was not laid off with much taste, nor was it large." George Washington was judging the garden with a ruler calibrated on grand plantation gardens. Still, he was inclined to stop at Bartram's again that September, a botanical distraction during a week when he was especially homesick for Mount Vernon.

When Benjamin Latrobe, an architect who would later work on the Capitol as well as the building and grounds of the executive mansion, visited Mount Vernon in 1796, he described its gardens in his journal. "On one side of this lawn is a plain kitchen garden. On the other a neat flower garden laid out in squares and boxed with great precision." Latrobe was unimpressed.

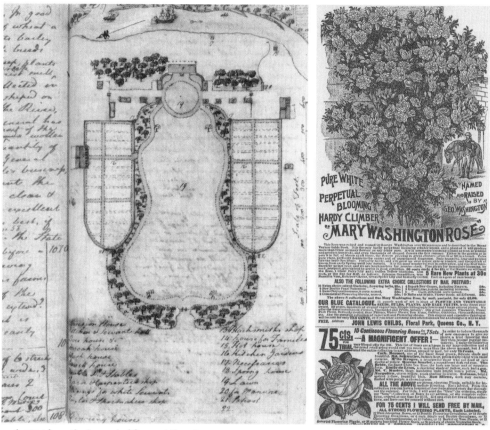

A page from the journal of Samuel Vaughan, an English merchant who visited Mount Vernon in 1797 and drew this plan of its gardens.

This advertisement from an 1881 *Ladies' Home Journal* is an example of American marketing moxie, as there is no evidence that Washington named a rose for his mother.

Of the geometric-patterned boxwood he sniffed, "For the first time since I left Germany I saw here a *parterre* stripped and trimmed with infinite care into the form of a richly flourished *fleur-de-lis*, the expiring groan, I hope, of our grandfathers' pedantry."

Yet we can forgive George Washington for garden elements that struck the chic Latrobe as old-fashioned. A teenaged Washington, during his first job as surveyor to Lord Fairfax, was a regular visitor to the Governor's Palace at Williamsburg. The gardens of the Virginia governor were known for their clipped boxwood formality. It is a rigid garden grammar: the ever-green nouns, the cut-and-shear verbs, the few adjectives provided by an infill of annual flowers or colored stones. Young George, ambitious and impressionable, must have banked the memories of these parterres for his future use.

As well as emulating the top-tier gardens of his youth, the president had personal reasons for his clipped fleur-de-lis. The victory over the British was still in recent memory, and the French, prominently the Marquis de Lafayette, had been America's knights in shining armor. After the war Washington and Lafayette remained close. The latter named his only son for George Washington who had no children of his own. It touched the president's heart. So it seems a small thing for Washington to have a French gesture in his flower garden for the occasional visit of the Marquis.

While now proudly independent as a nation, America and its culture were still in the strong gravitational pull of Europe. George Washington imported gardening books for his library including *New Principles of Gardening* by the whimsically named Batty Langley, and Philip Miller's *Gardener's Dictionary* of 1763, the go-to book for horticulturists of the day. Langley, a surveyor like Washington, wrote, "The most noble and pleasant situation of all others, is that on the top of a hill . . . where the air is fine and clear, with noble views. . . . All kinds of fenny, boggy, marshy lands, &c. whence fogs and noisome vapours arise, are always to be avoided." These were British horticulturists writing for an English audience. All well-to-do gardeners in the United States stocked their libraries with European books on the topic, as there were no substantive American gardening books yet.

Any eighteenth-century American gentleman worth his salt improved the land as an honorable pastime. Henry Middleton on his vast plantation near Charleston and William Paca of Annapolis were two such gentlemen. Each created terraced pleasure grounds, "falls" gardens, with the land sculpted into wide descending tiers. The platform effect showed off the residence, a sort of ornament atop a wedding cake. It enabled fine prospects, valued for aesthetics as well as good air circulation, as Batty Langley had noted.

It required a huge outlay of energy, this cutting and filling, to grind down the rough edges of nature. Humans, most of them African slaves, labored with axe, spade, and barrow. Draft animals hauled carts piled with

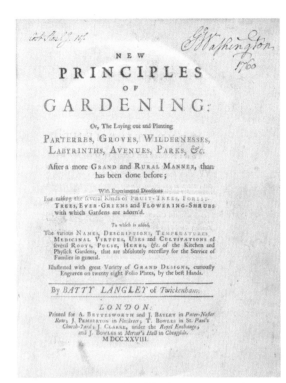

Langley's *New Principles of Gardening* was a regular source of design ideas for American gentlemen including George Washington.

Gentlemen gardeners in America often sited their houses on high ground and terraced the descents to river or road. Small slave quarters and other workshops—blacksmiths, coopers, carpenters—are built into this hill with mill and dock at the river's edge.

soil and stone. It was gardening as demarcation; here is improvement, there is wilderness.

The terraces at Middleton Place, still advertised today as the "First Landscaped Garden in America," step down to a pair of identical man-made lakes that stretch like butterfly wings toward the Ashley River. In Annapolis, Paca used perspective tricks to make his long view, from the garden's entrance to the summerhouse, appear longer. He crafted openings through trees and narrowed the planting beds in each successive level. These are gardens of the Age of Enlightenment, based on the geometry of classical proportion. The gentry learned their Latin and Greek and saw themselves as the new Romans, implementing a republic that would avoid the pitfalls of empire. The formality in their buildings and their gardens reflected a philosophical idealism of the day.

George Washington wanted classical designs for the new Potomac city as well, and he knew the man who could deliver. Among the presidential appointments were commissioners to supervise the work, surveyors, and an architect. Though today "L'Enfant" is best recognized as a stop on the Washington Metro, architect Peter (Pierre) L'Enfant set the footprint of the capital.

Born in France, L'Enfant studied art in Paris until, aged twenty-three, he crossed the Atlantic, part of an idealistic band of volunteers that joined America's revolutionary forces. He served as a military engineer under Lafayette and later as a major on Washington's staff. After the war he stayed on. In New York City, L'Enfant made his reputation as an architect remodeling Federal Hall into a massive temple of a building. He got wind that Congress was preparing to lay the foundation "of a City which is to become the Capital of this vast Empire," and in September 1789, he wrote to George Washington to volunteer his services as city planner. Burning with ideas, he was confident, almost brash—and he got the job.

Jefferson, as secretary of state, laid out the agenda for L'Enfant, or tried to. A letter itemized the work: planning, design, and site preparation for the major government buildings using "models of antiquity which have had the approbation of thousands of years." Thomas Jefferson had in his back pocket, so to speak, his own sketch for the city. His design was simple squares, not unlike William Penn's 1682 plan for Philadelphia or James

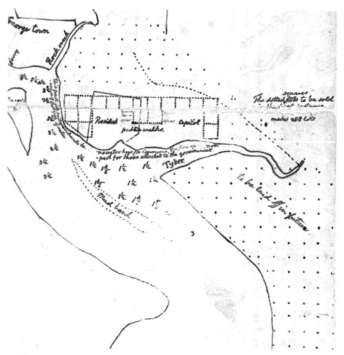

Thomas Jefferson's sketch for the layout of the federal city.

Oglethorpe's 1733 layout of Savannah. Or, as Jefferson was well aware, the grid that ancient Roman engineers applied when extending their empire. (Earlier in his career while a delegate to the Continental Congress, Jefferson had set up the grid system that eventually applied to the rectilinear state, county, and farm boundaries across the Midwest and western United States.) In Jefferson's quick rendering of the federal city, he placed the government buildings on a single line separated by public walks. The president's house rated two squares, as did Congress.

But L'Enfant had bigger things in mind. Grand gardens would connect an enormous presidential residence "with the publique walk and avenu[e] to the Congress House in a manner . . . as grand as it will be agreable and Convenient to the whole City." The executive and legislative branches would be separate but balanced, geographically as well as politically. Going over Jefferson's head, L'Enfant wrote directly to the president that, "the plan Should be drawn on such a Scale as to leave room for that aggrandisement & embellishment which the increase of the wealth of the Nation will permit it to pursue at any period however remote."

Here is a bird's-eye view of the city as seen by L'Enfant: the diamond-shaped district, ten miles on a side, one hundred square miles total, is split into four quadrants. At the center of his plan rises the Capitol atop Jenkins Hill, described by L'Enfant "as a pedestal waiting for a monument." The president's house stands a mile and a half distant on a crest above the river. In the address of the White House, 1600 Pennsylvania Avenue NW, the "NW" or Northwest refers to L'Enfant's original map.

George Washington sited the executive mansion himself. Rather than place it in a direct line with the Capitol, he followed Batty Langley's advice and set it on a rise with an expansive view. In June 1791 the president marked

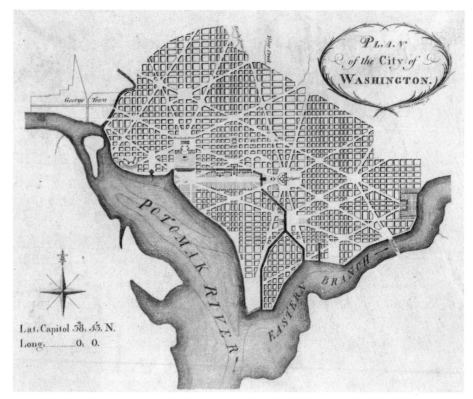

Peter L'Enfant's plan for the federal city.

George Washington supervising White House construction,
as imagined by American illustrator N. C. Wyeth.

off the land for the mansion with the eye of an experienced garden designer. L'Enfant was in tow. The following week L'Enfant wrote Washington a letter, saying that the new residence would combine "the convenience of a house and the agreeableness of a country seat situated on that ridge which attracted your attention at the first inspection of the ground." The president would command a view of some ten miles of the Potomac, a view toward Mount Vernon. A nearby navigational canal would convey commerce from the river to the city markets. The excavation of the canal offered opportunities to terrace the grounds "to procure to the palace . . . a prospect of the Potomac . . . which will acquire new sweetness being had over the green of a field well level and made brilliant by shade of few tree[s] artfully planted."

That L'Enfant calls the president's house "the palace" reflects his background. His models were monarchical, places like the French king's complex at Versailles, his boyhood town, and the Tuileries Palace garden near his school at the Royal Academy in Paris. L'Enfant also considered the plans of an array of continental cities via maps supplied by Jefferson—Frankfort and Amsterdam, Milan and Marseilles.

L'Enfant applied these lessons. He laid out the presidential grounds on cardinal points. What we call the West Wing and the South Lawn are aligned with their respective compass bearings. The design of the presidential garden is clearly on axis, slicing through the center of the house as it often does in landscape design, joining exterior and interior. This centerline of the garden intersects at a right angle with another axis that runs through the Capitol building, that monument to the rule of law.

Not every angle on L'Enfant's plan was at ninety degrees. Great diagonal avenues burst through the grid coordinates of the streets, connecting major buildings the way the Constitution united the states. At Versailles, radiating avenues were called *patte d'oie* for their resemblance to a goose's foot. For the new American city, L'Enfant explained that the diagonals would contrast with the general regularity and "afford a greater variety of pleasant seats and prospect." Views were important to L'Enfant, and eventually his undoing.

L'Enfant proved himself too much the *artiste*. He bickered with the commissioners and threw tantrums if one presumed to alter his plans. The president was conflicted. He saw the genius in his former staff member, if only L'Enfant could control his temper. But when the architect had the partially completed house of a commissioner's cousin dismantled because it was ruining one of his sight lines, he crossed the line. Peter L'Enfant had violated the rules of civility. On the 27th of February 1792, Thomas Jefferson fired him in a coolly worded letter dispatched from Philadelphia.

L'Enfant's plan persisted. The surveyors picked up, no doubt with a combination of relief and trepidation, where he had left off. Roads were laid out. Plots for private homes were sold in an orderly fashion. An architect,

James Hoban, won a contest for the design of the president's house. Workers cut sandstone for it and other government buildings at a quarry on Acquia Creek, forty miles down the Potomac. Barges carried loads of stone upriver with the tides. Avoiding transportation, brickmakers dug pits and built kilns on the presidential grounds. The requisite abundance of clay gives a hint of the soil that gardeners would eventually have to deal with at the White House.

George Washington had his mind on plants. In March 1792, he ordered more than two hundred trees and shrubs for Mount Vernon from Bartram's Philadelphia nursery. The order was a gardener's dream—get a catalog in the mail and request one or more of every plant listed. When Washington ordered in such quantity, it is easy to suspect that he might have been auditioning plants for the president's garden in the federal city.

The order included a tree discovered by William Bartram in Georgia and named for Benjamin Franklin (*Franklinia alatamaha*), never found again in the wild, and ironwood, a small tree named at the time *Jeffersonia egrilla*. (It wasn't until 1879 that the first president was similarly honored by having his name transformed into the palm genus *Washingtonia*.) Washington selected plants from states north and south of the Mason–Dixon line: moosewood from the Appalachians, bald cypress from southern swamps, and the Carolina sweet shrub. The Bartram brothers waxed poetic about white pine from the New England woods. "Magnificent! [the pine] presides in the evergreen groves," read the catalog. George Washington ordered six. It was as if the president hoped that the Congressional representatives from the fifteen states—Vermont and Kentucky had been added during his first term—could get along if their plants could co-exist in a garden.

Political mudslinging might be thought of as an early offshoot of American gardening, and George Washington was not immune. Even John Adams got into the act. He claimed that Washington "raised the value of his property and that of his family a thousand percent at an expense to the public of more than his whole fortune." Perhaps he was right. Washington had always been a good judge of real estate, and he did build some spec houses on land purchased in the District. Still one can hardly blame George Washington for wanting a short commute to what he had to anticipate would be frequent post-presidency consulting work. After turning over the reins to

Pinus Strobus

The white pine, a denizen of the northeastern forests, was planted by George Washington at Mount Vernon and by later presidents at the White House. From *A description of the genus Pinus* by A. Lambert, 1832.

John Adams in 1797, he was clear that he preferred to be "under my own Vine & Fig tree, as I do not think it probable that I shall go beyond the radius of 20 miles from them." The mileage to the federal city was only fifteen.

In retirement George Washington kept an eye on the progress of his now eponymous capital. (Fortunately the suggestion for "Washingtonople" had been ignored, and the commissioners settled on the simpler and shorter name.) Perhaps if he had lived to see the turn of the new century, the development of the city and its gardens might have moved along more quickly. Washington wrote a week before he died, frustrated "by the obstructions continually thrown in its way—by *friends* or *enemies*—[this] City has had to pass through a firey trial—Yet, I trust will, ultimately, escape the Ordea[l] with eclat."

A bit like Moses and the Promised Land, Washington did not live to see the president's house occupied nor its gardens planted. He died at Mount Vernon on December 14, 1799, sixty-seven years old. Two days earlier, he had caught a chill riding in miserable weather. He had been inspecting improvements to his land.

Founders’
Grounds

⁓

We have not the least fence, yard,
or other convenience.

ABIGAIL ADAMS to her daughter Nabby, November 1800

1800–1809

(1797–1801) JOHN AND ABIGAIL ADAMS
(1801–1809) THOMAS JEFFERSON

T HE MARYLAND ROAD was thick with trees, and the carriage driver was worried. His principal passenger was the president's wife. Mrs. Adams was stoic but clearly put out at being lost south of Baltimore for hours en route to the federal city. The leaves were turning, not the bright colors of Massachusetts sugar maples, but dull maroons and browns that suited her mood. Abigail Adams was not in a forgiving frame of mind when she described her arrival in a letter to her daughter Nabby. "Woods are all you can see from Baltimore until you reach *the city*, which is only so in name. . . . In the city there are buildings enough, if they were compact and finished, to accommodate Congress and those attached to it; but as they are, and scattered as they are, I see no great comfort for them."

Comfort, Adams was convinced, would have been delivered to the house if New Englanders had been in charge. "Very many of the present inconveniences would have been removed," she declared, as if the Puritan work ethic could have saved the day. Yet she couldn't help but be charmed by the "grand and superb scale" of the house with its view of boats plying the waters to Alexandria. "It is a beautiful spot, capable of every improvement, and the more I view it, the more I am delighted with it."

John Adams had arrived on the first of November 1800; Abigail Adams two weeks later. They occupied the new executive mansion in the new city a month ahead of schedule, a schedule set by Congress in the Residence Act

The wilderness surrounding the federal city as Abigail Adams encountered it, in a painting from 1801.

ten years earlier. Lest we think that this was a shining example of the federal government completing its first major project on time, only six rooms in the gigantic residence were any semblance of finished.

Earlier in his term John had written from Philadelphia to his "Dearest Friend," as he addressed Abigail in his letters. He moaned about his presidential workload and sighed, "I must go to the Federal City—that must be my farm in future, and I shall have as much more plague as less Pleasure, in it, than I had in the Quincy farm." In his usual conscientious manner he added, "Except that all the pleasure of life that is solid consists in doing one's duty."

In 1788 John and Abigail had moved from their first home, a saltbox at the foot of Penn's Hill, across town to Peacefield, a more elegant gentleman's farm, in Quincy, near Boston. With its fields, orchard, barns, and garden, Peacefield was typical of prosperous New England farmsteads in the late eighteenth century. Between the house and outbuildings, the space formed a yard or yards, workplaces filled with sounds of splitting wood and smells of laundry boiling with lye soap, butchering, not to mention a steaming pile of compost. In his diary on September 8, 1796, John Adams had recorded the day's activities in Quincy, "Sullivan gone for Seaweed. Bass and Thomas carting Manure from the Hill of Compost in the Yard. Billings and Prince laying Wall. Brisler and James picking Apples and making Cyder. Stetson widening the Brook." That in American English we still call the space around the house the "yard" (in England it is "garden") speaks to the value, linguistic and otherwise, placed on utility.

New England gardens were fenced to keep the livestock out, as early village law stipulated common grazing. At first, simple palings, stripped branches or saplings sharpened to points at one end, were stuck into the ground to make enclosures. As the decades passed and wealth increased, rustic palings and rail fences gave way to elegant pickets and ornamental gates; modest flower beds morphed into patterned boxwood-lined borders.

But these garden improvements had not reached the grounds of the president's house by the time John and Abigail Adams moved in. There was no yard, no walls or fencing. The house was drafty and the plaster still wet on the walls. Firewood was strangely in short supply, given the woods surrounding the city. As she lacked a drying yard, Abigail Adams strung up the laundry in the unfinished audience room.

We might have expected Abigail and John Adams to have an extensive garden at the president's house. They would have appreciated an ornamental garden as well as one to supply the kitchen. While minister to France in the early 1780s, he had strolled the gardens of the Tuileries and Versailles, "a very pleasant Amusement, and instructive Entertainment," when he could shoehorn in the time. She later joined him for a golden interlude where, with two of their grown children, Nabby and John Quincy, they occupied a manor house in the rural village of Auteuil.

Abigail Adams spent delicious hours in the garden—*le jardin*—at Auteuil, with its summerhouse, flowers, fishpond, and fretwork trellising. Thomas Jefferson was a frequent, favorite guest. In 1785, as they were packing to leave Auteuil for London where John would be the first American minister to Britain, Abigail wrote her niece Elizabeth Cranch, "I shall mourn my garden more than any other object which I leave." With her letter, Adams enclosed some seeds. "You will not get them early enough for the present Season, but plant and preserve them next year that I may find them blooming when I return." Cranch must have been a dependable garden caretaker for the saltbox home Adams termed her "Humble Cottage at the foot of the Hill." Be it ever so humble she would be happier still if a hint of her French garden followed her home.

From England, Abigail Adams sent Elizabeth's sister, Lucy, a fashion magazine and a garden book. The fashion magazine went viral. "*Gentlemen and Ladies, all borrowed it.*" Lucy kept the garden book in reserve. "The Treatise upon gardening, we have not had time to read, I think it must be entertaining. When I have read it I suppose I shall wish to have an ornamented Farm, at present our best way is to have a useful one." While it isn't clear which gardening book Adams had sent, it was touting the latest styles. An ornamented farm—the French called it *ferme ornée*—was what the posh gentry of England were building in the eighteenth century. Perhaps Abigail Adams had sent a copy of Thomas Whately's *Observations on Modern Gardening*, a guidebook of sorts, as well as a treatise on the latest designs. Both John Adams and Thomas Jefferson owned the book.

Jefferson joined the Adamses in England, his copy of Whately in hand. It was April 1786, an English spring of green grass and singing birds. During a lull in diplomatic activity, the two men set off in a post chaise from London to see for themselves the modern landscapes Whately discussed: Woburn and Caversham, Stowe and Blenheim, the ornamented farm at Leasowes.

"But ground is seldom beautiful or natural without variety, or even without contrast," Whately preached. French formality was being ousted in favor of a new English landscape style. It was the rise of romanticism. Gardens were composed to look natural even though entirely manmade. Parterres were dug up. Hills were built, vales excavated. Instead of rectangular canals, naturalistic lakes adorned with peninsulas, islands, and cascades were the thing, edged by winding walks. For eye-catchers there were "follies," features built to ornament the grounds: fake classical temples, faux Gothic ruins, monuments, obelisks, perhaps even a hermitage.

John Adams found these gardens "the highest entertainment" but questioned their purpose. "The Temples to Bacchus and Venus, are quite unnecessary as Mankind have no need of artificial Incitements, to such Amuzements. The Temples of ancient Virtue, of the British Worthies, of Friendship, of Concord and Victory, are in a higher Taste." He contrasted these built landscapes to American scenes. "Nature has done greater Things

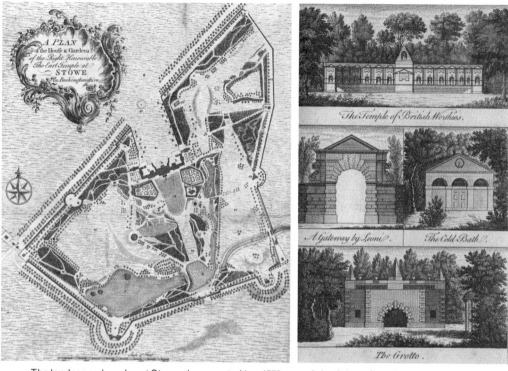

The landscaped garden at Stowe, documented in a 1773 map, was part of the Adams-Jefferson itinerary.

John Adams found the Temple of British Worthies, dedicated to people famous for ideas and actions, more to his liking than faux shrines to the ancient gods of wine and love.

and furnished nobler Materials there. The Oceans, Islands, Rivers, Mountains, Valleys are all laid out upon a larger Scale."

Jefferson took down more details, as was his wont: features, staff requirements, acreage. His diary entries extended to measurements of bridges and a sketch of a water mechanism that intrigued him. At Caversham, he wrote, "This straight walk has an ill effect. The lawn in front, which is pasture, well disposed with clumps of trees." John Adams and Thomas Jefferson in 1786: two American sightseers, two companions enjoying a garden excursion.

By 1800, everything had changed. When John Adams arrived in Washington his first term of office had nearly expired. He would not be staying in the president's house for a second term. His sometime friend, Thomas Jefferson, defeated him in a bitter race. Abigail Adams made an arboreal comparison, calling her husband an "old oak," deep-rooted, long-lived, and immovable, and Jefferson "a willow." The president and Mrs. Adams returned to Quincy as soon as his term ended in March 1801. They did not stay for Jefferson's inauguration.

Thomas Jefferson, America's patron saint of gardening, is justifiably famous for his gardens at Monticello. Over the course of his eight years in the president's house, given his usual horticultural enthusiasms, his gardening output was small. Digging deeper, his issue wasn't lack of interest but political philosophy.

Americans were worried about monarchs. "Avoid palaces and gardens of palaces," William Thornton, a Washington city commissioner warned, "If you build a palace with gardens I will find you a king." As Lucy Cranch told her aunt, Abigail Adams, "Luxery and extravagance are taking hasty strides through our Land, if not soon checked they will prove our ruin." The citizens of this young republic, just free of English kings, peered over the pond to France where a revolution starting with *Liberté, Egalité, Fraternité* ended with the guillotine and Napoleon Bonaparte. The widely circulated L'Enfant plan with its palatial presidential quarters was now suspect.

Jefferson stood for small government. He was bounded by budget and avoided federal debt, ironic for a man whose personal finances were often precarious. He outlined the grounds around the president's house first with a rail fence, then with a wall and gate, limiting its territory. He cut off seventy-plus acres that L'Enfant had designated for the presidential palace, designating it as a more democratic public common. That left five acres to constitute the grounds of the house (which later expanded to eighteen acres). On one side Jefferson's fence defined a private space for the country's chief executive—what is the South Lawn today. On the other side he established an entryway, a public face to the residence. In effect, Thomas Jefferson created the president's front and back yards as we know them today.

Jefferson was focused on buildings rather than gardens in the unfinished city. He appointed architect Benjamin Latrobe, the same gentleman who had criticized George Washington's Mount Vernon parterres, as Surveyor of Public Buildings. They worked on the Capitol. They added colonnades to extend the president's house toward the departmental offices on each side and a triple-arched entrance gate at the end of Pennsylvania Avenue to the east. But mostly they worked toward "rendering the President's house habitable." Among many problems, the roof still leaked.

Habitable or not, Jefferson lived in the president's house. He was alone in the federal city, without family except for the occasional visit from children and grandchildren. By the time he swore the oath of office, he was a widower of twenty years. There were servants of course, a French steward, an Irish coachman, and slaves from Monticello. To cope with his chief-executive-sized workload, he hired an army officer, Meriwether Lewis, as a secretary and aide. "Capt Lewis & myself are like two mice in a church," Jefferson wrote his daughter Martha, in May 1801.

They worked in Jefferson's study. The book-lined room, the "cabinet" as he called it, had maps aplenty—including, one hopes, those retrieved from L'Enfant—a globe to spin, charts to peruse. Always a gadget lover, Jefferson kept a small set of garden tools among the implements on his desk. He filled the room's windows with flowering plants arranged on a variety of stands. Geraniums and roses bloomed in the sunny recesses, scenting and softening the room.

Among the plants hung a cage for his mockingbird, Dick, the first in a long series of presidential pets to share the house and garden. Dick was

A mockingbird from *The Birds of America* by John James Audubon.

A scarlet geranium like those Jefferson grew, shown in an
1801 portrait by Rembrandt Peale of his brother Rubens.

a lively bird, sometimes loud, whose repertoire of Scottish, French, and
American tunes supplemented the usual birdcalls. Perhaps he sang accom-
paniment to his owner's violin. Jefferson had a "peculiar fondness" for
mockingbirds, wild and caged. He called them superior beings and warned
children at Monticello that they would be haunted if they disturbed the wild
nests. Dick whistled and warbled while the roses and geraniums bloomed.

The geranium, now almost a garden cliché, was a relative newcomer to
American horticulture. A novelty. It is related to our native perennial geraniums, such as the wild cranesbill, *Geranium maculatum*. Though by 1789
botanists had separated it into its own genus, *Pelargonium*, in America the
old common name stuck. First imported to Britain in the 1700s, it hails from
South Africa, carried back by Portuguese and Dutch traders as they made

their way around the Cape of Good Hope from India and the Spice Isles. To Jefferson, geraniums brought their own hope—sight and smell, red petal and aromatic leaf—to cheer his solitude.

Jefferson was an early windowsill gardener. Small window panes—glass was handmade and expensive—and lack of uniform indoor heating meant that tender plants were a rarity reserved for the rich. Jefferson clearly got a taste for the hobby, as it was during his presidency that he contracted for his own greenhouse to be built at Monticello. "My green house is only a piazza adjoining my study, because I mean it for nothing more than some oranges, Mimosa Farnesiane & a very few things of that kind."

His small greenhouse reflected Jefferson's general preference for simplicity. William Dunlap, a playwright and artist, recounted an impromptu meeting with Jefferson in the president's house: "He converses with ease & vivacity, possessing true politeness, which places his guests perfectly at their ease. During the short period which we pas[sed] with him, rendered shorter by the certainty of having interrupted him in study or Business (for he came into the room en dis-habille & slippered) he talked of the early approach of spring, of gardening French & English, prefering the latter & praising their great taste in laying out their ground." He and Dunlap also discussed hearing the first song of the frogs in the Washington wetlands on the south side of the executive mansion that season.

While Jefferson preferred English gardens, he favored a French chef, as well as French wine. One guest described his table as "republican simplicity . . . united to Epicurean delicacy." Gone were the "levees," the court-like audiences that presidents Washington and Adams had held weekly. Instead he invited guests to join him at a small oval dining table. And they were no doubt delighted with his vegetables.

Thomas Jefferson loved vegetables. While in office he made a study, summarized in an inked bar chart of striking neatness and precision, of produce available in the Washington markets. Columns mark the month; rows list the type of vegetable or fruit. The variety is impressive, with almost forty items listed. It is a clear illustration of seasonality with only three—lettuce, parsley, and spinach—available year-round. The local farmers who supplied the green markets in the District took advantage of the mild winters, but must have provided some kind of shade to extend their salad crops

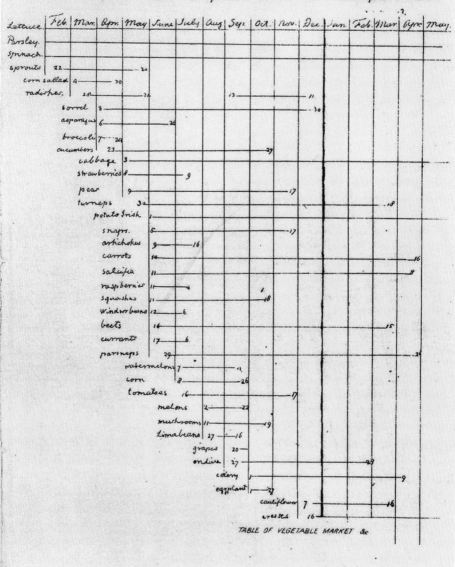

Jefferson's chart of the first and last appearance of produce in the Washington markets from 1801 to 1809.

through the heat of the mid-Atlantic summers. Jefferson, an avid fruit and vegetable gardener at home in Monticello, did not grow them at the president's house; he had too many building projects underway. But he took the time to study them, an example of the close observation and record keeping that marked the age.

Botany and horticulture were part of natural philosophy, that all-encompassing study of the physical world that burgeoned in the enlightened eighteenth and nineteenth centuries. Nature observed; nature described. England had its Royal Society, so why not America? Benjamin Franklin with others, including nurseryman John Bartram Sr., founded the Philosophical Society in Philadelphia in 1743. By 1787 it was called The American Philosophical Society for Promoting Useful Knowledge, and each of the first four presidents—Washington, Adams, Jefferson, Madison—were members. Plants were part of the common stock of knowledge to be cultivated. Exploring the botanical wealth of North America was a priority.

In 1793, Jefferson worked with the Society to raise funds for a French botanist, André Michaux, to explore the territory west of the Mississippi River. Michaux, who had arrived in America as the French king's botanist in 1785, had been busy. He had befriended the Bartram brothers, established propagating gardens in Hackensack, New Jersey, and Charleston, South Carolina. He had visited George Washington at Mount Vernon and Henry Middleton at Middleton Place. He had collected in Spanish Florida, as far north as Hudson Bay, as far south as the British Bahamas, and west in the United States to the Mississippi. But when he ventured to explore the Missouri basin under the aegis of the Philosophical Society, Michaux became embroiled in international affairs upon which the expedition foundered. Instead of concentrating on botany, he began acting as an agent for France— literally an *agent provocateur*—recruiting men to rid the Louisiana Territory of the occupying Spanish. At Jefferson's insistence, his government recalled Michaux to Paris.

Ten years later, in 1803, Jefferson went back to the members of the Philosophical Society, asking them to prepare his secretary and former frontier army officer, Meriwether Lewis, for a new western expedition. (That same year, Jefferson had doubled the size of the country via the treaty with France now known as the Louisiana Purchase.) The purpose of the expedition

White Oak.
Quercus alba.

Jefferson-sponsored expeditions documented plants
that would later shade the White House, including
Quercus alba. From *The North American Sylva*, published
by André Michaux's son, François André, between 1817
and 1819.

was commercial and political, but also scientific. Andrew Ellicott, one of
the original surveyors of Washington D.C., taught Lewis the rudiments of
map making. Benjamin Smith Barton from the University of Pennsylvania
tutored him in botany. Lewis and his handpicked co-leader, William Clark,
set out with their company in May 1804. They did not disappoint. They sent
back dried plant specimens, many new to botanists. They also sent back
seeds, which Jefferson distributed to expert gardeners in his circle. At least
one plant discovery from the Lewis and Clark expedition, the golden currant or *Ribes aureum*, was eventually grown on the White House grounds.

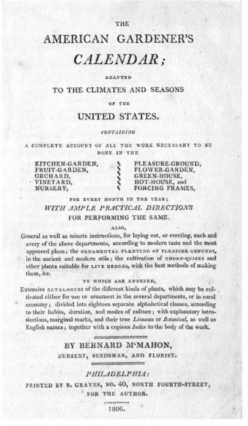

THE

AMERICAN GARDENER'S

CALENDAR;

ADAPTED

TO THE CLIMATES AND SEASONS

OF THE

UNITED STATES.

CONTAINING

A COMPLETE ACCOUNT OF ALL THE WORK NECESSARY TO BE
DONE IN THE

KITCHEN-GARDEN,	PLEASURE-GROUND,
FRUIT-GARDEN,	FLOWER-GARDEN,
ORCHARD,	GREEN-HOUSE,
VINEYARD,	HOT-HOUSE, and
NURSERY,	FORCING FRAMES,

FOR EVERY MONTH IN THE YEAR;

WITH AMPLE PRACTICAL DIRECTIONS

FOR PERFORMING THE SAME.

ALSO,

General as well as minute instructions, for laying out, or erecting, each and
every of the above departments, according to modern taste and the most
approved plans; the ORNAMENTAL PLANTING OF PLEASURE-GROUNDS,
in the ancient and modern stile; the cultivation of THORN-QUICKS and
other plants suitable for LIVE HEDGES, with the best methods of making
them, &c.

TO WHICH ARE ANNEXED,

Extensive CATALOGUES of the different kinds of plants, which may be cultivated either for use or ornament in the several departments, or in rural
economy; divided into eighteen separate alphabetical classes, according
to their habits, duration, and modes of culture; with explanatory introductions, marginal marks, and their true *Linnæan* or *Botanical*, as well as
English names; together with a copious *Index* to the body of the work.

BY BERNARD M'MAHON,

NURSERY, SEEDSMAN, AND FLORIST.

PHILADELPHIA:

PRINTED BY B. GRAVES, NO. 40, NORTH FOURTH-STREET,
FOR THE AUTHOR.

1806.

McMahon's breakthrough book.

Another, *Mahonia*, was named for Bernard McMahon who became one of
Jefferson's gardening confidantes.

Thomas Jefferson's extensive library—it later formed the kernel of the
Library of Congress—included many European books. But on April 17, 1806,
a book from Philadelphia arrived on the president's desk along with a letter:

> Sir.
>
> I have much pleasure in requesting your acceptance of one of my pub-
> lications on Horticulture, which I forward you by this mail. Should my
> humble efforts, meet with your approbation, and render any service to my

adopted and much beloved country, I shall feel the happy consolation, of having contributed my mite to the welfare of my fellow man. I am Sir,

With sincere esteem, and best wishes, yours, &c. Bernard Mc.Mahon

McMahon was an Irish immigrant, a horticulturist whose book, *The American Gardener's Calendar*, was the first substantial gardening book by an American author. After receiving a note of acknowledgment from the president, McMahon sent him tulip bulbs. Jefferson responded with some Mediterranean seeds and asked for some tarragon, if available. McMahon sent a few roots. They cemented a gardening correspondence with plants.

During his two terms Jefferson connected the president's house to the Capitol—slowly being completed on his watch—by grading Pennsylvania Avenue and planting trees on either side. There was room for improvement. Albert Gallatin, Jefferson's secretary of the treasury, described the scene to his wife: "swamp intervenes, and a straight causeway, which measures one mile and half . . . , forms the communication between the two buildings. A small stream, . . . decorated with the pompous appellation of "Tyber," feeds without draining the swamps." Tiber is the name of Rome's river; this particular stream had been known as Goose Creek before L'Enfant's time. Gallatin continues, "along that causeway (called the Pennsylvania Avenue), between the Capitol and President's House, not a single house intervenes or can intervene without devoting its wretched tenant to perpetual fevers." Small wonder that Jefferson put this roadwork high on his priority list.

Which street tree would he choose? In 1803, he wrote to a gardening friend in France, Madame de Tessé, "I have not been permitted to enjoy much those fine poplars of which you used to speak with such rapture." He wouldn't put off that enjoyment for long. That same year, he proposed planting them along an improved Pennsylvania Avenue, making a visual connection with the Capitol.

The Lombardy poplar is familiar to anyone who has visited the French or Italian countryside or has seen those landscapes rendered in art. The tree's columnar outline builds the form and background of so many southern European gardens. Now it seems like a strange choice for Jefferson to have made for the capital city, as it has turned out to be short-lived in the United States, but it was popular in the early history of street tree plantings in America.

Pennsylvania Avenue and its Lombardy poplars, looking toward the Capitol before the addition of its dome, around 1813.

The Woodlands, William Hamilton's Philadelphia estate, in a hand-colored engraving from 1809. A detail appears on page 32.

Another gardening friend of Jefferson's, William Hamilton, first brought the poplar to his estate, The Woodlands, in Philadelphia in the 1780s.

Jefferson called The Woodlands landscape, "the only rival I have known in America to what may be seen in England." Hamilton sited his estate on a high rise above the Schuylkill River, about seven miles north of Bartram's nursery. On a visit to England in the years after the American Revolution, he had been smitten with all things gardening. Having both motivation and means, Hamilton returned to his Pennsylvania estate and laid out a garden of winding walks opening to views of the city and the water. He assembled a prodigious assortment of plants from home and abroad. Michaux, who visited The Woodlands in 1802, called the collection immense. In addition to exotics, Hamilton grew all of the trees and shrubs native to the United States that could tolerate Philadelphia's winters. From China, he acquired the first ginkgo trees in America, both male and female, as if he were some sort of horticultural Noah. And he introduced the Lombardy poplar from Europe.

At The Woodlands visitors admired the Lombardy poplar's texture and its ability to provide a quick screen. For a street tree, it had the added benefit of a narrow, upright form. It was easy to propagate from cuttings—the tree does not form female flowers, and thus does not set viable seed—and nurserymen quickly added it to their offerings. By 1798, the William Prince nursery offered ten thousand of them. It was the perfect street tree for Jefferson's Pennsylvania Avenue project in Washington, especially as funds were running short and oaks, which were his preference, were more expensive.

Even as the young city was taking shape, as late as 1805 the grounds at the president's mansion still seemed "undressed," as Benjamin Latrobe observed. Thomas Whately's advice may have seemed even more relevant, as he urged readers like Jefferson neither to leave their grounds "naked and neglected" nor to miss "the appendages incidental to his feat and fortune." For the seat of any gentleman of means, not the least the residence of a president, "some degree of polish and ornament is expected in its immediate environs." And that is precisely what Jefferson and Latrobe would plan.

In their design, Jefferson and Latrobe respected L'Enfant's formality and the neoclassical mansion designed by architect James Hoban. They flanked the radial sight lines on the north side with avenues of trees. L'Enfant would have called them allées. The carriage drive was simple, underscoring

Jefferson's republican ideals of direct and open government—a straight line connected to a perfect circle. The grand scale was maintained, and the practical function as well. The thirty-foot-wide roadbed allowed two-way traffic; the circular turnaround had a ninety-foot diameter. A gently curving pedestrian walk invited strollers along the north perimeter of the property. On the south side of the house, two linear flower borders outlined a rectangle that framed the facade. A sunken ditch with a flanking wall, called a "ha-ha," at the south end of the lawn kept livestock out of the garden.

But in the lower right quadrant of the plan, something new was afoot. A curving English romantic garden spilled out, with paths unwinding around an irregular wood. Clumps of trees provided that element of surprise, the garden visitors' views opening and closing. A hundred-foot semicircle was captioned "Garden." While it was not the first romantic garden plan

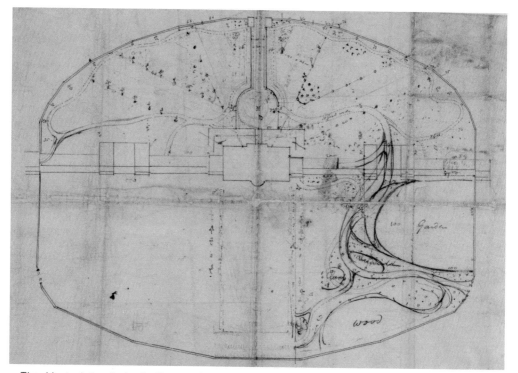

The oldest existing design for the presidential gardens and grounds, attributed to Jefferson and Latrobe, circa 1804.

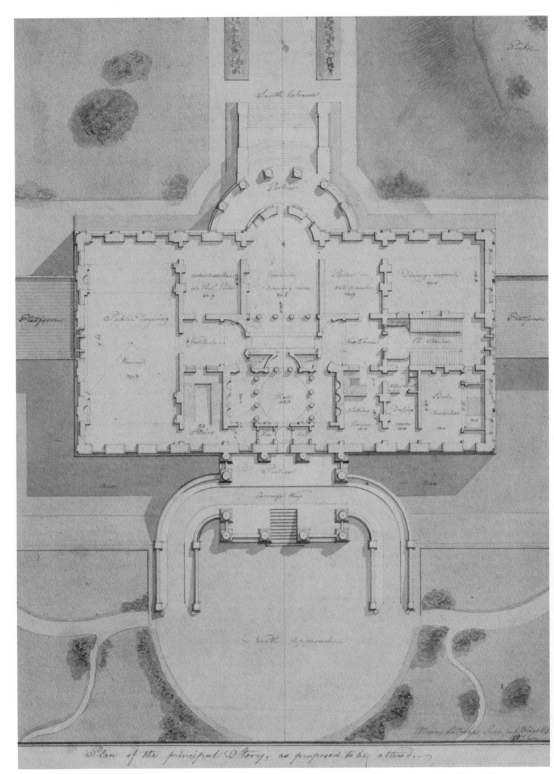

Latrobe's plan for Jefferson's first floor extensions shows some indication of the gardens. South is at the top, north at the bottom. On the upper right, Latrobe indicates a rise in elevation and labels it "Park" as in lands surrounding British country houses.

Latrobe's 1807 drawing shows, on the left, pedestrians at the South Portico looking over a hill planted with shrubbery to views of the Potomac and, on the right, a carriage at the North Portico's covered entry known as a *porte-cochère*.

in America—William Hamilton's Woodlands predated it, for example—it was certainly on the leading edge. If the radial axes and curving paths seem to make, like politics, strange bedfellows, perhaps it is because the design represents a transition. It is balanced on the scales between the classic and romantic in American garden history. At last we have the beginnings of what we now know as the White House garden.

Gentlemen's Occupation

❧

It stands on a public square and in a considerable garden.

JAMES FENIMORE COOPER, describing the 1826 White House in *Notions of the Americans: Picked up by a Travelling Bachelor*

1810s–1830s

D OLLEY MADISON NEEDED FLOWERS. Sitting at her writing table in the executive mansion, she put pen to paper and asked her Philadelphia friend, Phoebe Pemberton Morris, to find her some. They were not flowers to grow. "I will avail myself of your offer to chuse me a facinating Headdress," she wrote, "It must be of large size—I enclose you 20$ my darling, & you will add to the Bonit or Turbin, some artificial Flower or fruit for the Head." Dolley was not inclined to garden. As a hostess known for her parties as well as her turbans, she wrote Phoebe of her days busy at the president's house, "You will readily immagin my occupations—curteszing kissing &. &. our numerous acquaintances flock around us."

While Dolley Madison focused on fashion and decorating the interior of the house, James Madison turned his attention to the exterior. For the Madisons and their contemporaries, landscape gardening continued to be more of a gentleman's occupation than a lady's. With Jefferson's plan, James Madison would begin the garden in earnest.

It was time. Thomas Law, a real estate speculator in the city, left this description in 1811, tsking and shaking his head. "When I perceive the President's [house] unfinished, his garden in gullies & the rooms of his house unplastered; when the rain drips on my head through the roof of the Capitol; when I survey the neglected spot allotted to a garden which cost 30 Ds. P.

[dollars per] acre—I ask, can these disgusting scenes to strangers be pleasing to Citizens."

To turn the neglected spot into a pleasing scene, James Madison ordered ornamental plants. The oldest plant list for the executive mansion is dated March 31, 1809, a perfect time to start spring planting in Washington. It is a litany of selections "for Single trees"—specimens, that is—and "in line" for avenues. American natives like sugar maple and tulip trees joined British imports like the English walnut and English mulberry to create the formal front of the president's grounds.

Some privacy was wanted. Evergreens and understory trees appeared on the plant list, designated for "Close plantation & Clumps & for screens." With plants to add form and texture, President Madison's gardeners could start to form the swirls and shrubberies of the romantic corner of Jefferson's plan to the south and east of the executive mansion. While no construction documents exist, historians concur that the gardeners followed the Jefferson-Latrobe plan. It was a plan befitting a grand southern home and the Virginia plantation owners who were president for twenty-eight of the first thirty-two years of the nation's history.

Flowering trees and shrubs were part of the order. Redbuds and buckeyes bloomed, their colors set off by a dark backdrop of pines and hollies. Persian lilacs extended the season, blooming after the purple and white French varieties. Four kinds of rose of Sharon filled the summer border, with petals white, red, and striped. Roses were also on the list, though their variety and color went unspecified.

Local nurserymen supplied the plants to the president's gardeners. Thomas Jefferson probably recommended them, as he knew them all. Alexander Hepburn had done some custom propagation for Jefferson in 1801, including *Pesche Poppe di Venere*—Breast-of-Venus peaches—for Monticello. Theophilus Holt's connection was more pedestrian—he had supplied clover seed for the presidential lawn. Thomas Main was another local nurseryman, a Scottish immigrant who had settled two miles from Georgetown near Little Falls. His enthusiasm for American hawthorn led Jefferson to order hundreds of them for Monticello's hedges. The local nursery business flourished, horticultural entrepreneurs popping up like self-sowing annuals in spring, ready to supply the needs of the growing city.

Tulip trees, *Liriodendron tulipifera*, were among the first trees planted at the executive mansion. From *Vegetable Materia Medica of the United States* by Philadelphia physician and botanist William Barton, 1825.

Roses have been grown at the White House for more than two hundred years. From *Flora's Dictionary* by Elizabeth Wirt, 1855.

ALTHÆA.

Among the flowering shrubs ordered for the executive mansion were four varieties of althaea, botanically *Hibiscus syriacus*, now commonly called rose of Sharon.

Still, Madison was loyal to at least one out-of-town nursery supplier. While Benjamin Latrobe was in Philadelphia picking up furnishings for Mrs. Madison, he stopped by Bernard McMahon's shop on the east side of Second Street below Market. There he placed an order for vegetable seeds at the president's request. He likely transacted the business with the affable Ann McMahon, Bernard's wife, who managed the counter at the shop and later, after Mr. McMahon's death, took over the business.

With Latrobe's order comes a glimpse of the first documented presidential vegetable garden. What Madison's gardeners grew would supplement his table—at the time, presidents paid the expenses of feeding guests out of their own pockets. (Note that a half-cent coin was minted in Philadelphia from 1793 to 1857.)

Philadelphia June 27th 1809
Bought of Bernd. McMahon
3 c Early York Cabbage $1.12½
2 oz Early Battersea [Cabbage]   .75
2 oz Large late Battersea [Cabbage]   .50
1 oz Sugarloaf Cabbage   .37½
2 oz White Broccoli   1.—
2 oz Purple [Broccoli]   1.—
2 oz Green and Yellow Savoy   .50
1 oz Red Pickling Cabbage   .50
½ lb. Early frame Radish   1.—
½ lb. Salmon-coloured [Radish]   1.—
1 lb. Black & White Winter Radish mixed   2.—
2 oz Curled Endive   .50
2 oz Long prickly Cucumber   .75
3 oz Long orange Carrot   .37½
3 oz Long red Beet   .37½
3 oz Dutch Parsnip   .37½
½ lb. Norfolk Field Turnip   1.—
1 oz London Leek   .25
Box 25/100. Freight 50/100   .75
   $14.12½

This summer seed order was destined for fall planting in Washington. The vegetables would mature before the hard freeze or winter over for an early spring harvest. Many of the selections are root and cruciferous crops, good winter keepers, so we can assume that the president's grounds included a root cellar.

Bernard McMahon, ever willing to serve a new president, enclosed a letter apologizing that the peas, cauliflower, and salsify were, at present, unavailable. McMahon added, "I take the liberty of enclosing, in the parcel, a few of my Catalogues; you will much oblige me by distributing them." He closed with, "P S. The Box goes with this Mail Stage, and is addressed The President of the United States (Garden Seeds.)." An alpha address to be sure.

While the president received his seeds by the mail stage, this distribution was not typical across the new United States. Rural gardeners of the early 1800s saved their own seed, traded with neighbors, or relied on seeds of varying quality from itinerant peddlers. Enter the Shakers. The Shakers,

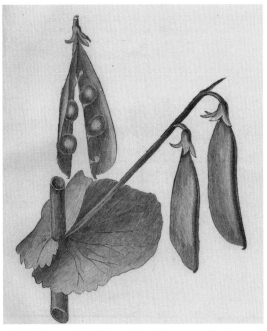

While Bernard McMahon did not have peas for the president in June 1809, seeds were likely obtained elsewhere as they were a favorite of Madison and Jefferson.

more formally the United Society of Believers in Christ's Second Appearing, were members of a religious sect with the unusual combination of communal living and celibacy. Adept at commerce, Shakers became synonymous with industry, craftsmanship, and honesty. In addition to the shaking dances of their worship, they shook up the American seed business. Their innovations were packaging, rigorous quality standards, and distribution.

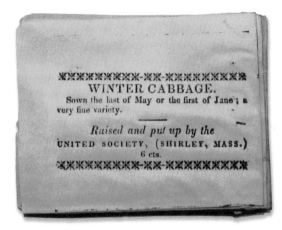

The United Society, commonly known as the Shakers, innovated the distribution of seeds, using standard printed "papers" or packets.

They invented the standardized paper seed packet. First individually hand cut and printed, by 1810 the technology-savvy Shakers improved the packet-manufacturing process with cutting tools and letterpress printers in their workshops. Shaker gardeners raised the seeds and collected, cleaned, and packaged them in their tidy communities strung across the country from Massachusetts to Kentucky. Their seeds were fresh, resulting in good germination rates, and grew true to the descriptions on the packets.

The Shakers created America's first organized door-to-door sales force, a force that reached an untapped rural market. A Kentucky farmer opening the door to a Shaker Brother had a choice of vegetable seeds not unlike the list that McMahon addressed to Madison. The Shaker peddler offered other products made in the Believers' workshops: woodenware, brooms, woolen and leather goods, wire sieves, packaged medicinal herbs and preparations. If you were the local general store proprietor, you could take one of the Shakers' wooden boxes of seeds on consignment. While Johnny Appleseed gets all the press, the Shakers had a bigger impact on food gardening.

James Madison knew of the Shakers. He was always interested in agriculture, both officially and personally. One day a letter arrived on Madison's desk from Elkanah Watson, a forward-thinking "scientific" farmer in Albany, New York. In his letter, Watson suggested a national board of agriculture. That idea took some time to implement; the U.S. Department of Agriculture wasn't established until Abraham Lincoln's administration. Watson went on to mention seeds he had received from the American consul at Naples, then "gave the shakers in this Vicinity—with an injunction to return me a partition of such seeds, as they might find new—& useful—& adapted to Our climate." The Shakers were "Faithful to their trust, they call'd lately & delivered me some Cabbage Seed of an intire new species in *this Country.*" Watson sent Madison a quarter of the seeds of this new Savoy cabbage "supposing you wou'd chearfully distribute a portion to some of your friends so as to promulgate a New & Valu[abl]e Article for the table."

Whether Savoy cabbage was on the menu is not known, but the table at the president's house was set on August 24, 1814, for an afternoon dinner for the members of Madison's cabinet and several officers. Two years earlier Congress had declared war on Great Britain. During the War of 1812, the "Second War for Independence," the U.S. Army made several attempts to invade Canada including the burning of present-day Toronto. In retaliation, the Redcoats were coming again, this time marching into Washington. As British troops approached the city that summer day, Dolley Madison watched troop movements with a spyglass from the roof. The president had ridden the eight miles to Bladensburg, Maryland, to monitor the battle, and she still hoped he would make it back in time for the meal. Wine, cider, and ale were set out in coolers when the president's bodyguard galloped up, waving and yelling that the Americans were in retreat.

It is worth noting that on this otherwise bad day, a gardener played a small but heroic role for posterity. Named Thomas Magraw, he helped to save the full-length Gilbert Stuart portrait of George Washington. As one of the Madisons' house slaves, fourteen-year-old Paul Jennings, described in his memoirs, the valet "and Magraw, the President's gardener, took it down and sent it off on a wagon, with some large silver urns and such other valuables as could be hastily got hold of. When the British did arrive, "they ate up the very dinner, and drank the wines, &c., that I had prepared for the President's party." Then they set the building on fire. By the dawn's early light of August 25, 1814, the president's house was a charred remnant.

The president's house with the sad remains of Madison's plantings after the British set it afire on August 24, 1814.

The war's tide soon turned. A peace treaty was signed. In Washington James Hoban, the original architect of the president's house, was hired back to rebuild it to original specifications. The house that took a decade to complete the first time was rebuilt in just over three years. James Monroe, who had served as both secretary of war and secretary of state under Madison, was elected president in March 1817. While construction on the president's house was winding down, the affable and low-key Monroe embarked on a fifteen-week goodwill tour, leaving Washington on the 1st of June.

The president traveled by stage and steamship, the latest mode of transport. On his tour, Monroe was greeted with pomp and parades. He was presented with bouquets of York-and-Lancaster roses, white and red, named for the parties in the English War of the Roses, now repurposed to signify the "Era of Good Feeling" between America's North and South in the wake of the successful war. Monroe visited well-known gardens along the way. In Waltham, Massachusetts, on July 7, he saw the "rich and highly cultivated grounds of T. H. Perkins" and "the costly and elegant enclosures of Mr. Lyman." And he stopped to have strawberries with Christopher Gore, an old and ailing friend from the diplomatic service.

Gore had brought a landscape gardener back with him from England who had laid out the grounds of Gore Place in the style of Humphry Repton. (Repton was an English landscape designer known for his broad, painterly designs.) With gently graded sweeps of lawn and the artful placement of trees, Gore Place had a park-like setting. As the White House grounds had not had a chance to mature, this description of Gore Place can serve as a placeholder for the design ideas of the day: "The carriage-turn, whole north side of the house is crowded with large trees; many Hemlocks, whose soft boughs sweep the ground at the edge of the drive, several Umbrella Magnolias among the Hemlocks, some large Lindens and many very tall White Pines. Just beyond is the flower garden, carefully sheltered and quaintly laid out in geometric fashion, with great banks of shrubs at the sides, plenty of smooth grass, and large beds crowded with perennials in rich, old-fashioned array."

Gardens do not fare well during construction projects. Back in Washington one can imagine the president's grounds once again pitted, pockmarked, and strewn with debris. To move things along, the now-retired James Madison gave up Charles Bizet, his longtime gardener from his Virginia home, Montpelier, to direct the garden restoration. Bizet planted gardens at the president's house from a plan, now lost, by Charles Bulfinch, the architect working on the Capitol. New plants stood out against the now bright white house, a heavy coat of white paint covering the stone charred in the fire. From then on the name "White House" stuck, although it took until Theodore Roosevelt to make it official. James Monroe officially reopened the house on January 1, 1818.

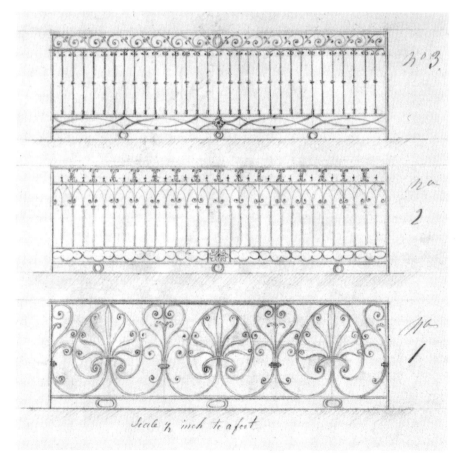

A receipt for Charles Bizet itemizes soil amendments, tool repair, the use of cold frames, and hand mowing.

Drawings for Paulus Hedl's elegant iron railings, circa 1818, with the anthemion or honeysuckle pattern on the bottom.

The new gardens at the White House sported a metallic addition. Paulus Hedl, an artisan in New York, had made wrought-iron entry gates and a railing for the north side of the house. Sparks flew from his anvil. Hammered and twisted into shape, the results were high craft. On the railings he used an anthemion, or honeysuckle pattern. On the gates he created fiddlehead curves unfurling like ferns, Greek keys and spear points, arrowheads, arches and trefoils. When Hedl arrived at the president's grounds, he installed two sets of double gates and two single, mounting them to sandstone gateposts built by stonemasons at work on the Capitol.

Only the president—and the wealthy—could afford this type of hand-made garden fencing or furnishing. But Hedl clearly had plenty of customers. As a contemporary wrote, "The demand for his wares soon rendered him rich; and now, instead of the monotonous parallelisms of straight iron rods, pierced through a single horizontal bar and pointed at the top, we have beautiful forms, which give so much elegance to iron railings as to cause us to forget their inhospitable intention." Hedl later patented one of his processes for ironwork.

The gates at the White House were meant to be decorative rather than inhospitable. They bordered the north entrance, reserved for official business, but unlike today the south grounds were open to the public. They were a place to stroll. Women in their bonnets, men in their top hats—one could see and be seen, take the air, all while enjoying the gardeners' efforts. The gates were an invitation, a reminder that the economy boomed, and that both partisan politics and sectionalism were, for a time, set aside. It was an era of good feeling in the garden, too.

When General Lafayette returned to America as the guest of the nation in August 1824, he hoped to "see for himself the fruit borne on the tree of liberty." In the forty years since Lafayette had helped the country achieve independence, both liberty and the land had been fruitful. Forests had been cleared and farms extended. Lafayette's secretary wrote, "The land in the interior is very productive, and so well cultivated, that the whole country appears like a garden."

Local dignitaries christened Lafayette Squares in New York City, Buffalo, and New Orleans as the general arrived on his thirteen-month nationwide tour. In North Carolina, he visited the town of Fayetteville, named

PRESIDENT'S HOUSE.

Strollers outside Hedl's gates on the north side of the White House were free to walk on the south grounds.

for him just after the Revolution. Perhaps Lafayette was amused when he arrived in the District of Columbia to find yet another square that would bear his name. Seven acres that had been part of President's Park to the north of the White House were officially rechristened Lafayette Square. It was early in the tradition of monumentalizing public spaces in America.

The writer James Fenimore Cooper was part of the welcoming committee for Lafayette in New York City. When Cooper visited Washington the following year, he saw a city just starting to pull itself up by its bootstraps. Standing on the steps of the Capitol, he had a view to the White House. Things weren't perfect, but Cooper conceded, "paved walks and a few scattered buildings, serve to give them something of the air of *beginning* to belong to the same town." Next to the presidential mansion and its garden, he noted the two executive office buildings "on each side of the 'white house' . . . having open courts between them." At one of Monroe's receptions Cooper reported, "The President's House is a neat, chaste building of the

An early painting of the White House and its new South Portico circa 1830, with the trees of Lafayette Square visible on the far left. From Anthony St. John Baker's *Mémoires d'un Voyageur.*

Ionic order, built of the same material, and painted like the Capitol." By that time the semicircular South Portico, designed by Benjamin Latrobe, had been added on to the White House, in the same way homes across America, both modest and grand, often added a porch that connected the residence with their surrounding grounds.

The next occupant of the president's house, John Quincy Adams, appreciated its considerable garden during his difficult term in office. From the start, the fifty-eight-year-old president faced an uphill battle. The 1824 election had been a fluke; Adams had received fewer popular and electoral votes than Andrew Jackson, but got in office by a squeaking margin in the House. There was no honeymoon period—Jackson's supporters started attacking him before Adams was even sworn in. After a long successful career as a diplomat, a Harvard Law School professor, and Monroe's secretary of state, John Quincy Adams must have been shocked to be depicted as the unpopular "professor" to Andrew Jackson's "plowman."

With the Adams administration came a new gardener, John Ousley. The twenty-something Ousley emigrated from County Wexford in Ireland in 1818 to the port of South Amboy, New Jersey. He might have been fleeing fever and hunger. A typhoid epidemic had reached that part of Ireland, and a season short on rain had also left a short harvest. America beckoned. By 1825, two and a half months after Chief Justice John Marshall swore in John Quincy Adams, Ousley was filing his naturalization papers with the Circuit Court of the District of Columbia, and on the 24th of May, John Ousley was sworn in as an American citizen. About that time, he became the gardener at the executive mansion.

There was plenty for Ousley to do. He tended the gravel walks and painted the picket fences, arbors, and trellises. He planted and weeded and pruned. To keep the lawns at least roughly trimmed, he arranged for mowers with scythes to cut the long grass for hay, and sometimes borrowed a flock of sheep. There were seeds to sow and cuttings to take for the cold frames and bell jars. And he put down his own roots. Ousley would stay in the position for decades, into the 1850s. The gardener had become part of the "B team," as civil servants sometimes call it. He would "Be" there after any given president was gone.

It was evident that the second President Adams, like the first, would be gone after one term. With his presidency faltering, John Quincy Adams was depressed. His father died. (Like something out of a novel, John Adams and Thomas Jefferson, reconciled in their later years, died on the same day—the fiftieth anniversary of the Declaration of Independence, July 4, 1826.) John Quincy wrote in his diary, "My health and spirits droop, and the attempt to sustain them by . . . botany, the natural history of trees, and the purpose of naturalizing exotics is almost desperate." Gardening was a personal act, so different from the burden of office. In the garden, he could suit himself.

He set out to learn with John Ousley as his instructor. He recorded the plantings. "In this small garden, of less than two acres, there are forest and fruit trees, shrubs, hedges, esculent vegetables, kitchen and medicinal herbs, hot house plants, flowers and weeds, to the amount I conjecture of at

The White House and its south grounds in 1831.

The first known image of a gardener at the White House, probably John Ousley, also shows the sheep sometimes brought in to assist with turf management, from an 1831 painting in the White House collection.

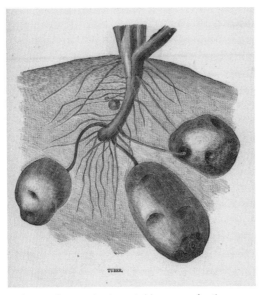

TUBER.

Among the esculent vegetables grown for the president's table were potatoes, a tuber that originated in the Andes, went to Europe with the Spanish, and came back to North America with later settlers.

least one thousand." Esculent, by the way, means edible. With gardening, there was always something new for Adams to study. "I ask the name of every plant I see. Ousley the gardener knows almost all of them by their botanical names, but the numbers to be discriminated and recognized are baffling to the memory and confounding to the judgment." Confounding or not, he was ready to learn.

He studied Michaux's *North American Flora* and the quarto volumes of *La Physique des Arbres* by the French physician-botanist Duhamel du Monceau. If only he had started sooner, Adams thought. Now, age fifty-nine, he regretted the decades gone. He might have mastered botany and dendrology as well as horticulture if only he had begun forty years earlier. The president consoled himself with a quote from Virgil, *Non omnia possumus omnes*. "We can't all do everything."

But garden he could, and enjoy the results. His was a garden that celebrated variety. "There are fruit trees in the garden, one red mulberry, several

This painting of a double peach blossom, labeled in John Quincy Adams's hand, gives a hint at the riches of the April garden at the president's house. Perhaps he intended to name the variety for his mother, A[bigail] S[mith] Adams, who had died ten years earlier in 1818.

With pen and paintbrush, President John Quincy Adams tracked his apple seed or "pippin" from planting in 1826 to the foot-tall seedling transplanted the following year in the White House garden.

Beeches, more Plumbs, a few cherries and three or four hazel nut shrubs," he wrote on the 18th of May. He cataloged the ornamental and the edible: "Of flowering trees one Tulip, now in bloom, a large weeping willow, one ash and one Florida Cornus dogwood, an Althea and a White-thorn hedge. Many Flowering Plants and culinary vegetables—Potatoes, Carrots, Beets, Radishes, Cabbages, Cauliflower, Lettuces, Peas, Beans, Jerusalem Artichokes, Onions, Garlick, Chives and Asparagus."

A burgeoning spring garden. On another day he noted sea kale, a perennial leafy vegetable that was common in early American vegetable gardens, and basil. He picked herbs, using texture and fragrance to fix them in his

When John Quincy Adams took his morning swims, he had a view of the White House in its picturesque setting.

memory. "I plucked this morning leaves of Balm and Hyssop, Marjoram, Mint, Rue, Sage, Tansy, Tar[ra]gon, and Wormwood, one-half of which were known to me only by name—the Tarragon not even by that." The diversity of herbs and vegetables was striking.

Now instead of his usual four-mile walk before breakfast, Adams took a quick swim—he called it a "bath"—in the Potomac and went directly to the garden. The results of his vigorous weeding will ring true to gardeners. "Our bath and the garden weeding occupied three hours of exercise, inducing back fatigue. I persevere in seeking health by laborious exercise, but with not entire success." And like all gardeners, new and old, he watched over his seedbeds of fruit and nut trees with the alertness of a new parent, "I sowed in my seed bed toward the east end of the garden 15 cherry stones. Continued weeding with the hand, the bed in which I sowed last November walnuts, chestnuts, pecan nuts, and acorns, none of which have yet appeared."

The following April, his patience paid off. "The Elm, Sycamore, Maple and Locust are beginning to unfold their leaves . . . The fig tree leaf is push-ing, and the bud at the top of one [of] last year's Shagbark is opening in each of my seedling beds. One new plum shows its kernel. One of my last year's apple trees has already grown up as much length of stem as it acquired in the whole of last Season—say four inches." Yet still he sighed over his "infant plantation" and the gauntlet of frosts and a hailstorm "which broke and lac-erated piteously most of their tender leaves."

Adams was not alone in his desire to increase his knowledge of botany and horticulture. The Washington Botanical Society, an early association of plant enthusiasts, had published *Florula Columbiensis: a list of plants found in the District of Columbia* in 1819. Agricultural societies had long existed; now horticultural organizations more focused on ornamental gar-dening were forming up and down the Atlantic seaboard. The Pennsylvania Horticultural Society was founded in Philadelphia in 1827; its Massachu-setts counterpart started two years later in Boston with John Quincy Adams as an honorary member. The Charleston Horticultural Society followed the next year in 1830.

Horticultural societies educated members through lectures and meet-ings and fostered competition with juried shows. By the mid-1830s at the annual horticultural exhibition in Washington, John Ousley pulled in prizes for produce grown on the White House grounds, including a silver cup made by Williams & Co. for his specimens of hautbois strawberries, artichokes, and a cabbage weighing eighteen and a half pounds.

Books and periodicals by Americans and for American gardeners were coming off the presses at increasing rates. *The American Gardener*, written by John Gardiner and David Hepburn and published in Washington in 1826, brims with flowers as well as vegetables, including "cockscombs, tri-colours, egg plants, globe amaranths, balsams." (The "egg plants" referred to are a yellow and white annual, *Limnanthes douglasii*, rather than the vegetable.) The recitation of flowers, peppered with names ranging from mythological to suggestive, continues with "lobels' catchfly, sweet sultans, lupines, white and purple candy tuft, flos Adonis, dwarf poppy, Venus' navelwork, Venus' looking glass, virgins' stock."

But beyond plants esculent and floral, John Quincy Adams favored trees. In Baltimore he picked up acorns from a white oak on the battleground

John Ousley grew prizewinning strawberries in the White House gardens.

FLORULA COLUMBIENSIS:

OR A

LIST OF PLANTS

FOUND IN

THE DISTRICT OF COLUMBIA;

ARRANGED ACCORDING TO

THE LINNÆAN SYSTEM,

Under their respective Classes and Orders, &c.

AND

EXHIBITING THEIR GENERALLY RECEIVED COMMON NAMES,

AND TIME OF FLOWERING,

During the Years 1817 and 1818.

WASHINGTON:

PRINTED FOR THE WASHINGTON BOTANICAL SOCIETY.

BY JACOB GIDEON, JUN.

1819.

Florula Columbiensis is an example of the work accomplished by early horticultural societies.

at North Point, fought just after the White House had been burned, and brought them back to plant in his nursery. He collected chestnuts and elm samaras, planted them, and monitored their growth. He was "answering the great ends of my existence" with his trees. He could see the whole of nature in the leaves and branches of his saplings. Watching them "with a view to ascertain some of her laws," Adams anticipated Emerson's essay "Nature" which would be written ten years hence and Thoreau's stay on Walden Pond in the mid-1840s.

Adams had an environmental objective, "to preserve the precious plants native to our country from the certain destruction to which they are

John Quincy Adams planted acorns, nuts, and other tree seeds in the nursery beds behind the White House.

tending." Agriculture and commerce had taken their tolls on the eastern forests. Like any parent with a calling, he wanted to pass it on to his offspring. He exhorted his eldest son, George Washington Adams, to "acquire the relish for the occupations which the cultivation of long-lived trees require." John Quincy Adams was planting a legacy of trees.

While president, Adams launched the country's first forestry project, as a renewable supply of lumber for the Navy. The next generation of shipbuilders would, given his plan, have access to hundreds of acres of oaks growing in Florida. (Adams had negotiated the acquisition of Florida from Spain in 1819 while he was secretary of state under Monroe.) The coastal live oak, *Quercus virginiana*, was his species of choice. It was prized for the tensile strength of its wood and an angled branching structure that was literally ship-shape. "Old Ironsides," the USS *Constitution*, had been built of live oak. In 1827, a tract of land in Florida's panhandle on Santa Rosa Sound near Pensacola was cleared and planted. Although politics soon sidetracked the effort, and iron soon overtook wood for warships, some of the live oaks planted for President Adams still grow today.

In residential gardens across the Deep South, the live oak was a prized ornamental. Majestic avenues of live oaks, draped with Spanish moss and adorned with mistletoe and resurrection fern, are etched in the national consciousness. What would Scarlett O'Hara's Tara have been without them? About the time that Adams's designees were planting his live oaks near Pensacola, Martha Turnbull in Feliciana Parish, the cotton frontier of Louisiana, was measuring out and planting acorns that would mature to the live oak avenue that continues today to usher visitors into Rosedown Plantation.

Live oaks don't thrive as far north as Washington, but a more adaptable southern arboreal icon, the bull bay magnolia, arrived with the next

This portrait of Andrew Jackson is one of the few images of Jefferson's entry arch (removed in 1857) with its flanking willows, south and east of the White House.

The bull bay or southern magnolia, from eighteenth-
century British botanist Mark Catesby's *Natural History of
Carolina, Florida and the Bahama Islands.*

Jackson must have planted his magnolias after the inauguration, as the White House and its grounds
were mobbed for the event in 1829, shown in this illustration by British illustrator Robert Cruickshank.

administration. In 1828 General Andrew Jackson won the election hands down. Jackson had always loved a good fight, and he carried the dueling scars and a number of embedded bullets from various battles to prove it. This war hero would now ride triumphant into the presidency. But "Old Hickory," as his troops had called him, had a soft spot. His beloved wife, Rachel, died suddenly, just as they were getting ready to leave The Hermitage, their home near Nashville, for the inauguration. If White House lore serves, Andrew Jackson brought magnolia saplings from Tennessee as a memorial to her. They were planted on the south side of the White House, close to the portico.

Jackson buried Rachel in her Hermitage flower garden. Two years later he built a small circular temple over the grave. This tempietto, a small circle of classical columns capped with a dome, was not an unusual garden feature—James Madison had one built to hide his ice house at Montpelier—but its application as a funerary monument, particularly in a garden, and the

Andrew Jackson's Hermitage in Tennessee, with the tempietto built as a memorial to his wife, Rachel.

memorial planting of magnolias at the White House are signposts to a new trend in American horticulture: the landscaped cemetery.

A century before, dealing with the dead was straightforward. Your loved one was interred in the churchyard or in a designated graveyard on the family farm. (The grounds on which George Washington sited the executive mansion had just such a burial plot on the old Pearce land.) As decades piled up, so did the dead. At the same time that church graveyards, especially in populated areas, were running out of room, older attitudes toward death were being elbowed out by new sensibilities.

A kinder and gentler resting place was wanted, a Paradise replete with gardens as well as angels. Lydia Maria Child, an American writer on topics ranging from abolition to household management but best remembered for the poem "Over the River and Through the Woods," wrote, "We ought not to draw such a line of separation between those who are living in this world, and those who are alive in another." She offered some design advice. "So important do I consider cheerful associations with death, that I wish to see our grave-yards laid out with walks and trees, and beautiful shrubs, as places of public promenade." Death's sting, softened by plants and planting design.

A new word, "cemetery," derived from the Greek for "sleeping place," came into common parlance. America's first landscaped "sleeping place" was Mount Auburn Cemetery. Six miles outside of Boston on a hilly, eighty-acre site in Cambridge, it was dedicated in 1831. The Massachusetts Horticultural Society had a hand in its development. With its water features, specimen trees, and winding walks, it looked like a public garden. It attracted thousands of visitors; Boston added a public horse-drawn trolley from the city center to accommodate the crowds.

Mount Auburn ignited the spark, and across the country cities and towns of any size established landscaped cemeteries in the next decades. In Philadelphia a group of investors bought the core of the old William Hamilton estate, which morphed into The Woodlands Cemetery Company. In Washington, Glenwood Cemetery opened in 1854. James Hoban, the original architect of the White House, is buried there.

The curves, trees, and water features of Mount Auburn Cemetery outside of Boston, in a mid-nineteenth-century painting by Thomas Chambers. A detail appears on page 54.

Embellishments

❧

We have the most beautiful flowers &
grounds imaginable, and company &
excitement enough, to turn a wiser head
than my own.

MARY TODD LINCOLN in a letter to Hannah
Shearer, a Springfield, Illinois, friend, 1861

1840s–1880s

(1837–1841) MARTIN VAN BUREN

(1841) WILLIAM HENRY HARRISON

(1841–1845) JOHN AND LETITIA TYLER (DIED 1842),
  THEN JULIA TYLER (MARRIED 1844)

(1845–1849) JAMES AND SARAH POLK

(1849–1850) ZACHARY AND MARGARET TAYLOR

(1850–1853) MILLARD AND ABIGAIL FILLMORE

(1853–1857) FRANKLIN AND JANE PIERCE

(1857–1861) JAMES BUCHANAN

(1861–1865) ABRAHAM AND MARY LINCOLN

(1865–1869) ANDREW AND ELIZA JOHNSON

(1869–1877) ULYSSES AND JULIA GRANT

(1877–1881) RUTHERFORD AND LUCY HAYES

(1881) JAMES AND LUCRETIA GARFIELD

(1881–1885) CHESTER ARTHUR

EW OF THE presidents who immediately succeeded Andrew Jackson made significant changes to the White House grounds. To be fair, some of them ran out of time. William Henry Harrison served only one month because, it is said, he caught a chill during his two-hour inaugural address, the longest on record, during which he failed to wear a coat and hat. He died. A bit later, James Polk added a statue of Jefferson, whom Polk esteemed for his expansionist policies, to the North Lawn. So, let us fast forward to the next major designer who came to the White House.

One indication of Andrew Jackson's widespread popularity was that parents started naming their babies after him. One of those, Andrew Jackson Downing, grew up to be as popular a garden designer as his namesake had been a politician. By 1850, when President Millard Fillmore invited him to make recommendations for the White House grounds and public spaces in Washington, everyone knew Downing's name.

Downing was born into the business—his family ran a nursery in Newburgh, New York—but his ambitions and abilities went beyond retailing plants. He wanted to refine America. A precocious lad, he published his first essay, "Rural Embellishments," at age sixteen, and went on to launch a magazine, *The Horticulturist*, a journal of "Rural Art and Rural Taste." Handsome, affable, and glib, he took English gardening concepts from sources

Gardeners added wooden trellises, picket fences, and arbors to the White House grounds, and President Polk brought Jefferson's statue from the Capitol rotunda in 1848. The statue was returned to the Capitol in 1874.

like his London counterpart John Claudius Loudon, with whom he corresponded, and gave them a lively American slant.

Even our weather seemed more energetic. "The ugly words of English gardening are *damp, wet, want of sunshine, canker*," he wrote. "Our bugbears are *drought, hot sunshine, great stimulus to growth, and blights and diseases resulting from sudden check*." He brimmed with enthusiasm for his countrymen. "With us," he continued, "a feeling, a taste, or an improvement, is contagious; and once fairly appreciated and established in one portion of the country, it is disseminated with a celerity that is indeed wonderful, to every other portion."

In 1841, ten years after his garden writing entrée, Downing set out to disseminate his philosophy in book form. *A Treatise on the Theory and Practice of Landscape Gardening, Adapted to North America* was the first book on landscape design for a U.S. audience that combined theory, "the why," with

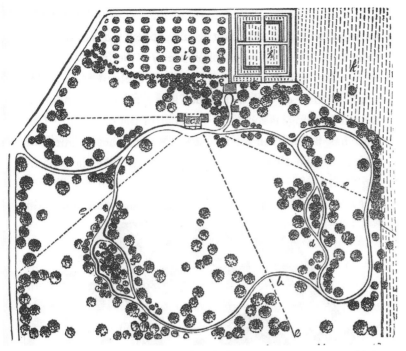

Downing's *Treatise* included this plan of an ideal picturesque country seat with the house separated from the utilitarian kitchen garden and orchard, and a curving drive surrounded by lawn, and wooded dells, punctuated by sight lines.

practice, "the how." An instant hit, it went through nearly a hundred editions and printings by the end of the century. It was dedicated to John Quincy Adams, "lover of rural pursuits," who was also the great uncle of Downing's wife, Caroline De Windt. Horticulture, then as well as now, was a small world.

Assuming President Fillmore read Downing's book—and many Americans did—he would have found planting styles divided into categories: the "beautiful," with simple formal lines, and the uneven, naturalistic "picturesque." Downing explained his concepts with an analogy of trees. "In nature we would place before the reader a finely formed elm or chestnut, whose well balanced head is supported on a trunk full of symmetry and dignity, and whose branches almost sweep the turf in their rich luxuriance; as a picturesque contrast, some pine or larch, whose gnarled roots grasp the rocky crag

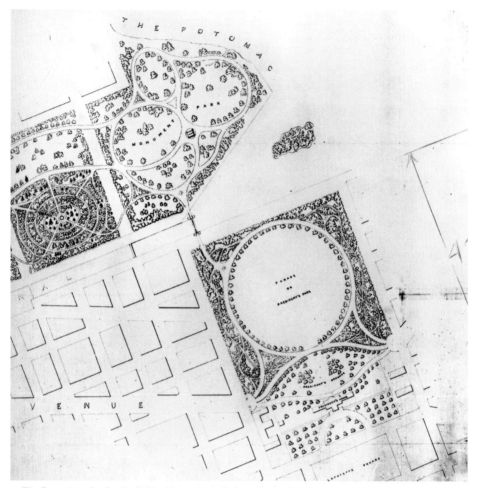

The Downing plan for the White House included regularly planted trees and an open parade ground surrounded by curving, densely planted shrubberies.

on which it grows, and whose wild and irregular branches tell of the storm and tempest that it has so often struggled against." He left room for architectural gardens near the house and promoted ornament—vases, sundials, seats—as proper embellishments for all types of landscapes. He endorsed conservatories for exotic plants.

Downing's plan for Washington and the White House grounds did, in fact, combine the beautiful and the picturesque. The Capitol would be flanked with an artificial lake and fountains alongside a botanic garden. He would frame the new Tudor castle of the Smithsonian and the Natural History Museum—described as "five acres under one roof"—with picturesque pleasure grounds and an evergreen collection. In President's Park, a round lawn would encourage public gatherings, encircled by an elm-shaded carriage drive and traversed by winding pedestrian paths. The lawn was the centerpiece, "the soft turf which, beneath the flickering shadows of scattered trees, is thrown like a smooth natural carpet over the swelling outline of the smiling earth." He sounds besotted.

If this reads like a city park near you, that is no surprise. Downing was a reformer, and public parks were at the top of his list. The landscaped cemetery had proved a draw. "If the road to Mount Auburn is now lined with coaches, continually carrying the inhabitants of Boston by thousands and tens of thousands," Downing wrote, "is it not likely that such a garden, full of the most varied instruction, amusement, and recreation, would be ten times more visited?" He waved the banner for parks as key institutions for a democracy, akin to public schools, libraries, and the ballot box. He advocated for agricultural colleges to teach American horticultural practices. He exhorted towns and villages to plant street trees, though he disliked Lombardy poplars. Instead, he wrote, "Select the finest indigenous tree or trees such as the soil and climate of the place will bring to the highest perfection." In short, plant native trees.

His design for the White House grounds was a formal grove of trees composed, one assumes, of varieties native to the Potomac's riverine environment. The design seems stiff, but perhaps Downing felt that the president's house required a dignified "beautiful" treatment. The site, as Abigail Adams had pointed out half a century earlier, spoke for itself. And Downing simply wasn't finished; "I have not shown on the plan several ideas that have occurred to me for increasing the beauty and seclusion of the President's grounds, because I would first wish to submit them for the president."

Submit them he would not. On July 28, 1852, Downing with some of his family set out on the first leg of the trip from Albany to Washington aboard the Hudson River steamer *Henry Clay*. Her captain, pulling out near a rival boat, the *Armenia*, set out to race downriver to New York City. Under full steam, the engine caught fire and sank near Yonkers, with eighty passengers

The south grounds as Downing would have seen them, with a simple greenhouse and small fountain.

lost. While Downing's wife survived, both he and her mother drowned. America's seminal landscape designer, the father of landscape architecture, flag waver for village improvement and urban parks, died three months shy of his thirty-seventh birthday.

Downing's detailed plans for the White House were lost with him that day on the *Henry Clay*, though his designs for the Mall and Lafayette Park went on to be implemented. His partner, architect Calvert Vaux, whom Downing had recruited from London, would go on to team up with Frederick Law Olmsted. They submitted the winning design for New York's Central Park five years later. Olmsted and his son, Frederick Law Olmsted Jr., will return to the story of the White House gardens in decades to come.

Some years after his death, during the Buchanan administration, Andrew Jackson Downing's ideas made a contribution to White House horticulture in the form of glass. Nowadays it is easy to take glass for granted, but in early America glass was dear in more ways than one. It was hand crafted, blown, and spun, and thus limited to about eighteen inches square. The number and size of windows in a building also drove federal tax valuation: the more and larger the windows, the higher the tax. The glass tax was repealed in 1847, roughly coinciding with industrial techniques for rolling plate glass. Glass and steam heat were about to democratize indoor horticulture.

Downing had seen the conservatory as genial, sweet-scented, and warm in winter "when all out-of-door nature is chill and desolate." He had recommended glasshouses for a specific segment of the population, "The many hours of pleasant and healthy exercise and recreation afforded to the ladies of a family, where they take an interest themselves in the growth and vigor of plants, are certainly no trifling considerations where the country residence is the place of habitation throughout the whole year." The women of the White House heeded his call, including the poised, intelligent, and much-admired Harriet Lane.

Harriet Lane could entertain. Her uncle and guardian, the courtly James Buchanan, our bachelor president who served from 1857 until 1861, invited her to live at the White House as his hostess. She'd had practice, learning the ropes in London while he was minister to Great Britain under Franklin Pierce. When the Prince of Wales visited the White House in 1860, the Marine Band dedicated their arrangement of "Listen to the Mockingbird" to Miss Lane. Perhaps the ghost of Thomas Jefferson's pet mockingbird, Dick, whistled along. "Halley" Lane was charming and vivacious. The newspapers loved her, and she loved flowers.

Buchanan indulged her with a proper conservatory. It replaced the orangery Andrew Jackson had installed for overwintering citrus and tender palms and that, in turn, Franklin Pierce had expanded into a greenhouse by trading its solid ceiling for one of glass in 1853. Harriet Lane's conservatory was a more elaborate affair, a high, ornamented glass sunroom devoted to the display of plant specimens. She could open double doors from the State Dining Room—the same room in which Jefferson had tended his geraniums—and step into a different world.

Breathe. The air had a quality, moist and rich, perfumed with citrus trees. Mysterious mouths of pitcher plants yawned. Aloes and cacti spiked. The plants in the White House conservatory created a compact world where jungle and desert, bog and scree all met. A journalist captured his impressions in 1858, "As you enter the conservatory itself it seems almost like penetrating the luxurious fragrance of some South American island, so warm

An early photograph documents the extent of the White House conservatories by the end of the 1850s.

and odiferous is the atmosphere. . . . Here you may see orange trees, and a lemon tree . . . rows of prickly cactus of every size and shape . . . camellia japonica, delicate spirea, ardisia, and poinsettia."

While it might have seemed like South America to this particular journalist, Harriet Lane's conservatory collection was an accidental ark, a global roundup of plants. Pitcher plants—*Nepenthes*—came from the Malay Archipelago, camellias were an Asian addition, and poinsettias (named for Joel Poinsett, a South Carolinian who, as first U.S. minister to Mexico, brought the plant home with him) arrived from Central America. The White House conservatory was a demonstration in miniature of the growing availability and desirability of unusual plants.

The nineteenth-century plant trade was driven by new transportation: clipper ships and steamships, canal boats and railroads. Energy, particularly the extraction of coal, fired boilers that created steam to power engines

This depiction of Harriet Lane's White House conservatory appeared in *Frank Leslie's Illustrated Monthly* in 1858.

as well as heat glasshouses. Other inventions helped. The Wardian case, a greenhouse in miniature, made plants mobile, enabling specimens collected on distant shores to arrive alive.

Plant trade was powered by expansionism. Britain's 1842 Treaty of Nanking had "opened" China to trade, including plant collecting. U.S. Commodore Matthew Perry did the same in Japan in 1854. What better place to display horticultural booty than in a glasshouse?

Newspapermen called the wood-and-glass conservatory "a most fitting addition to The White House." American homeowners followed suit. Conservatories, large and small, were being built into or added onto houses of all shapes and sizes. Emily Dickinson's father, who was elected U.S. Representative for Massachusetts in 1853, added a small one to his Amherst home for

At the Civil War White House a civilian, a soldier, and a boy lounge on the South Lawn and on Jefferson's wall, marred by graffiti. The wall was removed in 1873.

the pleasure of his two daughters in 1855. Emily Dickinson described it in a letter, "My flowers are near and foreign, and I have but to cross the floor to stand in the Spice Isles." Part of the lure of the glasshouse was its exoticism. Just as travelogues and explorers' tales were popular reading, a conservatory brought the romance of distant lands to the gardener's doorstep. Dickinson tended her conservatory until the end of her life; White House hostess Harriet Lane had to yield hers much sooner.

All gardens are ephemeral. Plants change with the seasons. They live and die in a larger cycle. Presidential gardens have another temporal overlay as their owners come and go by dint of the office. Harriet Lane's conservatory became Mary Todd Lincoln's on the same day that the reins of power transferred from James Buchanan to Abraham Lincoln in 1861.

And what a time. The Union was wrenching apart. A month after Lincoln's inauguration the Civil War began with bombardment of Fort Sumter

Azaleas bloom on the conservatory benches in this 1863 Mathew Brady photograph. This delegation of tribal leaders visited the Lincoln White House in an unsuccessful attempt to negotiate a settlement to the conflict with settlers in Kansas and the Colorado territory.

in Charleston harbor. Washington and its surrounds filled with troops. South of the White House gardens—what today is the Ellipse—the Army set up a cattle yard to supply meat to the encampments. Addressing the 166th Ohio Regiment one August day, gathered on the White House lawn, Lincoln said, "I happen temporarily to occupy this big White House. I am a living witness that any one of your children may look to come here as my father's child has."

While managing the war efforts, Lincoln took time to sign the Morrill Act in 1862. The act set aside a grant of 30,000 acres of public land for each state, the sale of which would fund "land-grant" colleges. These branches of learning would teach useful subjects related to "agriculture and mechanical arts." Think Iowa State and University of Georgia, Texas A&M, and Rutgers—all land-grant colleges. Land-grant colleges and the

U.S. Department of Agriculture, established the same year, generated the Extension Services and Master Gardener programs so familiar to gardeners today.

The gardens of the White House that Abraham Lincoln occupied were still regularly open to the public, though closed and patrolled at night for wartime security. Walt Whitman, who was a nurse in Washington Army hospitals between 1863 and 1865, attended one of the Saturday receptions, called "levees," and described "a compact jam in front of the White house— all the grounds fill'd, and away out to the spacious sidewalks." The six-foot-four president greeted the crowds, "drest in black, with white kid gloves, and a claw-hammer coat, receiving, as in duty bound, shaking hands." Whitman speculated on Mr. Lincoln's mood, suggesting that he looked "very disconsolate, and as if he would give anything to be somewhere else."

Mary Todd Lincoln would have been near her husband, no doubt adorned with flowers, as was her habit. She appreciated the White House gardens, and planned menus based on the fruits and vegetables grown on the grounds. To her friend Hannah Shearer, she wrote that she wished "I

Mary Todd Lincoln bedecked with flowers in 1861.

could hand you over the magnificent bouquet, just sent me, the magnolia is superb."

The two younger Lincoln boys, Willie and Tad, were the first children to live in the White House. Their parents were notoriously indulgent, and the boys had the run of the house and gardens. One of Lincoln's bodyguards left this description of their vast play area:

> The White House and its surroundings during wartime had much the appearance of a southern plantation—straggling and easy-going. On the east side of the house beyond the extension—since removed—which corresponded to the conservatory on the west, was a row of outhouses, a carriage-house and a wood-shed among them. Back and east were the kitchen garden, and the stable where the President's two horses were kept. South of the house was a short stretch of lawn bounded by a high iron fence. Still beyond was rough undergrowth and marsh to the river. North and to the west was a garden, divided from the rest of the grounds by tall fences. It was a real country garden, with peach-trees and strawberry-vines as well as flowers.

Willie and Tad could be a trial for the gardeners. Their pet goats developed a particular taste for flowers. The conservatory was another favorite haunt for the boys and their friends, Bud and Holly Taft. (The Tafts' father, Horatio, was an attorney at the U.S. Patent Office. If there is any relationship with later president William Howard Taft, it is distant.) The Taft boys' teenage sister Julia acted as informal babysitter for the gang. As a treat, Mrs. Lincoln would often send her off to the conservatory for "the bouquet man" to make up flowers for Julia to take home. Bouquets were a floral largesse, sent in place of a formal visit by the president's wife. Julia Taft described the bouquet maker's process: "He would take a perfect flower, rose, cape jasmine or Camellia and with his assistant tying the short-stemmed flowers on to broom straws, build up a structure of the size and shape of a cabbage, with an edging of forget-me-nots or delicate ferns. This was then put into a stiff paper bouquet holder and was ready for presentation."

The head gardener, John Watt, had his office in the conservatory wing. He was tolerant of the children, and kept goldfish, always an attraction, in the water lily tank. Watt had special fun teaching Miss Taft the "long Latinized names" of the rare plants in the collection. Yet Watt's knowledge of graft seems to have extended beyond the horticultural kind. Was he, as one historian put it, the "snake in the garden"? He and Mrs. Lincoln became enmeshed in garden-related fraud.

A hand-tied bouquet in the style of the
Civil War–era White House.

Raised a Kentucky belle, Mary Lincoln indulged in retail therapy. Big time. She shopped in Philadelphia, New York, and Boston. Her purchases for redoing the White House far exceeded the $20,000 allocated by Congress. As Watt had buying authority for plants, supplies, and labor, he padded bills to give Mrs. Lincoln wiggle room with her creditors. The "Manure Fund" assisted with acquisition of china, crystal, wallpaper, carpets, and paint. Mrs. Lincoln and Mr. Watt were widely criticized, particularly when a controversial State of the Union speech was leaked to the press in advance of its delivery, apparently through Watt's subterfuge. (He admitted to picking up the speech in Lincoln's office, memorizing sections, and passing them on to the press.)

Watt's horticultural duties had been suffering for some time. In 1860, a visitor to the conservatory had penned a scathing review. "Dirt and disorder, decayed leaves under potted half starved plants, met your view at every turn," wrote the anonymous critic in *The Gardener's Monthly and Horti-cultural Advertiser.* "Some shrubby plants had been, for want of pruning, allowed to grow as trailers; and the aquarium was filled with dirty, green, stagnant water, in the midst of which floated two leaves of an unhappy aquatic." The miserable aquatic was the giant *Victoria regia*, the queen of the water lilies.

Criticized for her own queenly behavior, Mary Lincoln always took John Watts's side. After he was dismissed as White House gardener in February 1862, he was appointed to inspect seed in Europe for the Patent Office, despite his reputation. Back in the United States the following year, he enlisted in the Union Army and served until the end of the Civil War.

Mary Lincoln's enjoyment of her fineries would be short. The city of Washington was an unhealthy place, especially for children. Mosquitoes from the swampy areas spread viral diseases like yellow fever, though that wasn't known at the time. Thousands of soldiers and horses were encamped around the Potomac, compromising the drinking water. The City Canal, envisioned by L'Enfant and George Washington as a commercial coup and constructed in the bed of the Tiber Creek south of White House, had, by the 1860s, devolved into an unused open ditch of runoff and sewage. The young Lincoln boys ran and played outdoors, no doubt attracted, as children are, to any kind of water. In 1862, both Tad and Willie Lincoln contracted fevers, probably typhoid, and eleven-year-old Willie succumbed. The poet Nathaniel Willis described him as "a wild flower transplanted from the prairie to the hot-house." The flowers that dressed his body were sweetly scented mignonette.

At night, Abraham Lincoln would often walk from the White House through the grounds to the War Department and its telegraph for the latest news from the battlefields. One night, a year after Willie Lincoln's funeral, Walt Whitman captured this scene:

A spell of fine soft weather. I wander about a good deal, especially at night, under the moon. To-night took a long look at the President's House—and here is my splurge about it. The white portico—the brilliant gas-light shining—the palace-like portico . . . the White House of future poems, and of dreams and drams, there in the soft and copious

Mignonette adorned the coffin of Willie
Lincoln. Here they are shown with carnations
or "pinks" in an 1851 floral dictionary published
in Philadelphia.

moon—the pure and gorgeous front, in the trees, under the night-
lights, under the lustrous flooding moon, full of reality, full of illusion—
The forms of the trees, leafless, silent, in trunk and myriad-angles of
branches, under the stars and sky—the White House of the land, the
White House of the night, and of beauty and silence—sentries at the
gates, and by the portico, silent, pacing there in blue overcoats—stopping
you not at all, but eyeing you with sharp eyes, whichever way you move.

Gas lamps, installed during James Polk's years at the White House, now
illuminated Lincoln's nocturnal walks, lighting the observations of both
sentries and poet.

In the months following Lincoln's assassination in April 1865, Whitman
wrote "When Lilacs Last in the Dooryard Bloom'd," an elegy to the fallen

president, the "western, fallen star," poignant with the image of a simple garden scene in its third verse:

In the door-yard fronting an old farm-house, near the white-wash'd palings,
Stands the lilac bush, tall-growing, with heart-shaped leaves of rich green,
With many a pointed blossom, rising, delicate, with the perfume strong I love,
With every leaf a miracle—and from this bush in the dooryard,
With delicate-color'd blossoms and heart-shaped leaves of rich green,
A sprig with its flower I break.

As well as conveying the elegiac relationship to Lincoln's death, Whitman might have been describing the lilacs in front of many homes in America. Perhaps the lilacs ordered by James Madison in 1809 still bloomed at the White House. They are long-lived shrubs.

The glasshouse at the White House, however, was short-lived, being continually modified. After Buchanan's old wood-and-glass conservatory burned—a flue burst on the southwest side on a blustery day in January 1867—Andrew Johnson replaced it with a bigger, better structure of glass and iron. Over ensuing administrations, the executive greenhouses kept growing as if in response to a horticultural manifest destiny. President Grant had his billiard and smoking room snugged up next to them so that while the gentlemen played, smoked, and chewed (aiming for the spittoons, one hopes, as well as the corner pockets), Mrs. Grant and the ladies could adjourn to her "garden spot of orchids." The president seemed to have a different use in mind, as an additional greenhouse was designated as a grapery with "a large number of the choicest vines having been already introduced into it."

The Grants also presided at the opening of the Centennial Exposition in Philadelphia's Fairmount Park on May 10, 1876. U.S. history had hit the triple digits. With one hundred years behind it, the nation realized it *had* a past, and was going to host an event to prove it. During its six-month run, nearly ten million visitors came through the entrance gates—about 20 percent of the U.S. population. It was the mother of all American world's fairs, its first official exposition. Officially titled the "International Exhibition of the Arts, Manufactures and Products of the Soil and Mine," it was awash with rarities.

THE WHITE HOUSE, FROM THE
CONSERVATORIES.

Panicled hydrangeas bloomed at the White House after the Civil War.

Hydrangeas were popular for American homes of
all sizes, including this one in Lincoln, Illinois, the
only town named for Abraham Lincoln before his
presidency.

Horticultural Hall on the day that President Grant opened the Centennial Exposition in Philadelphia.

The Horticultural Hall that President and Mrs. Grant toured that day was a Moorish confection. (Washington Irving's *Tales of the Alhambra* was popular at the time.) With its keyhole arches of polychrome masonry and vast clerestory windows, it was the largest conservatory ever built, larger than its predecessor, the "Crystal Palace," designed in 1851 for London's Great Exhibition. It is hard to imagine the jaw-dropping awe inspired by this glass expanse. It captured the sky. It floated over aquatic gardens and fountains. It enveloped a vast courtyard of palms and eucalyptus, bananas and giant ferns. Over the course of the Exposition, displays of horticulture—hyacinths and gladiolas, rhododendrons and chrysanthemums—vied for prizes and for gardeners' consideration. Outdoors, thirty-five acres of patterned gardens wound their way along Fountain Avenue.

Frédéric Auguste Bartholdi, the sculptor of the Statue of Liberty, fronted the main building of the exhibition with his thirty-foot cast-iron "Fountain of Light and Water." (The exhibit of the right arm of Liberty was a

The exotic plants were enthralling at the Exposition celebrating the one hundredth anniversary of the Declaration of Independence.

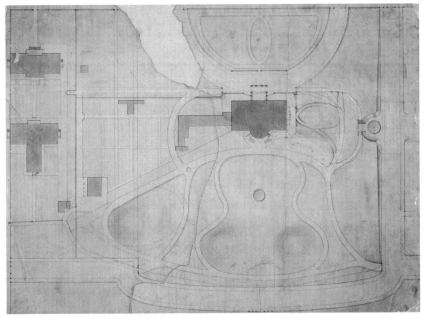

A site plan from around 1870 includes Grant's fountain on the South Lawn and reveals an extensive vegetable garden on the west side, before the construction of a new building to house the State, War, and Navy Departments. It also shows two artificial mounds that a Congressman named Ogle likened to "an Amazon's Bosom."

bigger draw. For fifty cents you could climb a ladder up the arm to the torch's balcony.) At the suggestion of Frederick Law Olmsted, Congress bought the fountain for $6,000 after the fair was over and installed it on the Capitol grounds. President Grant also added a fountain to the White House grounds, a seventy-five-foot-diameter round pool with a steam-powered jet on the South Lawn. American iron foundries made cast fountains and garden furnishings accessible to the buying public in general.

Meanwhile, when Rutherford B. Hayes came into the White House in 1877, Grant's billiard room went out. A conservatory extension took its place, now running the full width of the State Dining Room. Yet another glasshouse, this one for roses, was added. In summer, their fragrance would waft into open windows of the upstairs rooms.

In addition to eliminating billiards, President Hayes banned alcohol from the White House. Instead of offering drinks after a meal, he and Mrs. Hayes would lead the guests through the conservatories, hoping perhaps to

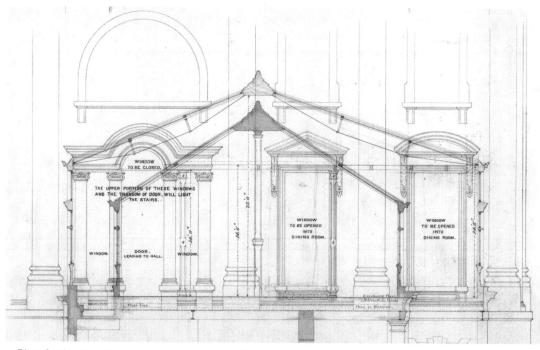

Plans for the new conservatory, opening onto the dining room.

Rutherford B. Hayes and Lucy Webb Hayes,
conservatory expanders and tree planters.

Plans for the rose house where gardeners forced hundreds of plants for flower arrangements.

One image from an early stereoscope of the interior of the White House conservatory with its mix of specimen plants, cast-iron urns, and a bench for resting.

evoke Eden before the Fall. After one such gathering, Secretary of State William Evarts smirked, "It was a brilliant affair; the water flowed like champagne." For her quiet efforts and soft drinks, Mrs. Hayes would later earn both the nickname "Lemonade Lucy" and the sincere appreciation of the Women's Christian Temperance Union.

Temperance leapt the White House fence and entered the public park. Newly installed water fountains encouraged passersby to quench their thirst with something other than alcohol. Henry D. Coggswell, a San Francisco dentist who had made a fortune fixing the miners' teeth and investing in mining stocks during the California Gold Rush, donated an outlandish dolphin-bedecked fountain for the nation's capital, installed at 7th and Pennsylvania in 1882. Throughout the coming decades, drinking fountains or "bubblers," the trademark coined by Kohler Water Works of Wisconsin, would become commonplace in parks across the country.

Glasshouses were also bubbling up from coast to coast. At the Capitol grounds, the United States Botanic Garden went from a one-bay Gothic greenhouse to a huge glass rotunda with five extensions. Golden Gate Park's Conservatory of Flowers went up in San Francisco in 1879. In St. Louis, Henry Shaw built his Linnean House for the Missouri Botanical Garden in 1882.

To superintend the White House conservatories, Hayes hired Henry Pfister from his home state of Ohio as head gardener in 1877. Pfister was born in Zurich in 1846, and he later mentioned having worked in Paris and London. If so, he started young. In February 1872, the twenty-five-year-old Pfister made the Atlantic crossing on the SS *Samaria* from Liverpool to Boston. He worked his way to Cincinnati, a boomtown on the Ohio River. It seems likely that Rutherford or Lucy Hayes met him there. Pfister was in his early thirties when he joined the staff at the White House, and he hit the ground running.

Amaryllis were a favorite of Pfister's. He ordered quantities of them for the White House and set off hybridizing—crossing different species to make new plants. Eventually the president's conservatories had one of the best collections in the country. One March, Pfister had a bit of a what's-in-bloom brag in *Gardening* magazine:

Amaryllis were hybridized and grown for display in the White House conservatories and in parlors across America.

The Amaryllis are a gay sight. *Rosa Bonheur, Mrs. F. Houk, vittata, majestica* and a host of other hybrids fill a long bench intermixed with ferns. *Ixora coccinea* six months old from the cutting is in bloom. *Hibiscus rosa sinensis* with young plants of *Gardenia citriodora* and forced plants of the blue flowered hardy plant *Baptisia australis* make a telling display. The large variegated leaved periwinkle (*Vinca*) is used in 5-inch pots as a hanging plant for the fronts of the stages, and it's quite easy to have it in flower at this time. A double flowered bramble, *Rubus rosaefolius* is grown extensively in pots and forced for early flowering.

It took a small army to maintain this fine indoor display. Payroll ledgers show Pfister, who worked seven days a week, supervising five gardeners, who worked a mere six. Four laborers shoveled the coal to run the boilers to make the steam to heat the air. William Fisher made the bouquets. Frank Thompson delivered them to designated recipients around the city with his horse and cart; later an Isabella Thompson took over for Frank, the only woman regularly employed at the White House gardens in those days. She was, according to census records, his mother.

Outdoors there were a garden foreman and laborers. Men painted fences and fountains, spread manure, weeded and trimmed, rolled the lawn, and performed a task that still falls to gardeners across the land—"abating nuisances"—although neither the type of nuisance nor the method of abatement was specified. Trees were planted, staked, watered, and whitewashed with lime to prevent sunscald. The horticulturists also set up for the annual Easter Egg Roll, a tradition started by the president and Mrs. Hayes, and cleaned up in its wake.

President Hayes had always been interested in history expressed through trees. He gets credit for instituting commemorative tree planting

Two participants in the Easter Egg Roll.

An 1874 map shows a manmade body of water, Babcock Lake, between the White House and the still unfinished Washington Monument. Built in the 1870s, the lake was a fleeting romantic landscape feature, filled in after First Lady Lucretia Garfield contracted malaria. South and east of the Monument are the Department of Agriculture's propagating greenhouses.

A detail from a Currier and Ives print shows the park-like setting of the White House, the partially completed Washington Monument, and the busy Potomac before the creation of the Tidal Basin.

at the White House. At Spiegel Grove, his home in Fremont, Ohio, Hayes had planted offspring of the willows from Washington's tomb at Mount Vernon, white oaks grown from acorns of Connecticut's Charter Oak, and tulip trees from James Madison's Montpelier. Since Hayes, presidents and presidential family members—with the help of able-bodied gardeners who do the heavy digging—have planted trees, leaving horticultural gifts for future administrations and generations. Perhaps Hayes was reflecting J. Sterling Morton's efforts in the brand-new state of Nebraska, where Morton started Arbor Day, first officially celebrated in 1874. (Morton would be appointed secretary of agriculture in the second Cleveland administration. His son, the founder of Morton Salt, was the namesake and original benefactor of Morton Arboretum near Chicago.)

South of the White House grounds, workers completed the Ellipse during the Hayes administration. And it was just in time, as a new focal point was rising to completion. The Washington Monument began as a private project in the 1840s. The ground was too swampy for its original site, so

After Garfield was shot less than four months into his term, well-wishers brought gifts for the president to the White House gates, everything from patent medicine to flowers.

President Arthur was fond of the conservatories, a fact employed by a *Puck* cartoonist in this botanical-political lampoon.

The view of the Monument from the South Portico over vine-covered railings, the fountain with its round basin, and the grounds, open daily to the public.

it was shifted slightly west, which is why it lines up perfectly with the Capitol but is off center to the White House. Progress on the obelisk languished due to mismanagement and lack of funds. The Civil War intervened, then the Army Corps of Engineers took over. Hayes saw the monument rise, as did James Garfield during his short, tragic presidency. (First Lady Lucretia Garfield contracted malaria and nearly died in May of her husband's first year in office. Two months later President Garfield was shot by an assassin then lingered, suffering, through the summer of 1881 until his death on September 19.) Garfield's successor, Chester A. Arthur, dedicated the Washington Monument in 1885. It is a white exclamation point in the skyline, and still the tallest structure in the city, a city that shares its name and honors the same man. First in war, first in peace, first thing you see looking south from the White House.

Gilded Gardens

∽

I saw some excellent examples of carpet bedding in the White House grounds, but I find in my notebook particular reference to two immense beds of crotons that in themselves amply repaid me for my visit. The beds were twenty-five feet in diameter, with about 350 plants in each, seventy-five varieties being represented altogether.

EDITOR, *American Florist*, 1888

1880s–1900s

(1885–1889) GROVER AND FRANCES CLEVELAND

(1889–1893) BENJAMIN AND CAROLINE HARRISON

(1893–1897) GROVER AND FRANCES CLEVELAND

(1897–1901) WILLIAM AND IDA MCKINLEY

(1901–1909) THEODORE AND EDITH ROOSEVELT

W HO DOESN'T LOVE a wedding? On Wednesday, June 2, 1886, at seven o'clock in the evening, President Grover Cleveland married Frances Folsom in the Blue Room. It was not the first White House wedding; various sisters and nieces, sons and daughters, and close friends had made use of the executive mansion as a wedding venue over the years. The Cleveland nuptials were notable as the groom was the first standing president to tie the knot under the White House roof. The fact that there was a twenty-seven-year age difference—journalists had been speculating that Cleveland was courting Frances's widowed mother—added tang to the reporting. It was fêted in the newspapers like a royal wedding and had flowers to match. Though the bride did not carry a bouquet, her gown was trimmed with orange blossoms and myrtle.

Head gardener Henry Pfister and his staff had been busy. The Blue Room was a bower, with potted palms grazing the ceiling, accented with groups of blooming azaleas, begonias, hydrangeas, geraniums, and roses, and over-the-top floral décor:

> Over the doorway a floral scroll of red, white, and blue bore the motto "E Pluribus Unum." Groups of plants, including begonias and hydrangeas in bloom, stood at each side of the room near the centre, and the fireplace glowed with a representation in flowers of a blazing fire. Upon the

east mantel there was a solid bank of pansies in different colors, with the letters "June 2, 1886," in white pansies across its length. Upon the mantel facing this one was a bank of roses, dark-hued ones at the centre, and graded to the lightest procurable hues at the edges, with the monogram "C. F." ["C" for Cleveland and "F" for Folsom] interwoven in moss and white roses.

If there were a Guinness Book of World Records marked "POTUS" (the official acronym for *President Of The United States*) and "FLOTUS" (*First Lady* . . . you get the idea), the Clevelands would have piled up several wins. Frances Folsom Cleveland, age twenty-one, was then and now the youngest first lady. She delivered the first baby born of a presidential couple in the White House: their second daughter, Esther (baby-number-one, Ruth, was born in New York between Grover Cleveland's two terms). Cleveland is the only person to have served two non-consecutive terms in the White House, which is why, as of the Obama administration, there have been forty-four presidencies but only forty-three presidents.

Two ladies pose on the lawn with a display of crotons in colorful contrast to the White House.

GROVER CLEVELAND,
President of the United States.

FRANCES C. FOLSOM.

The wedding picture of Frances Folsom and Grover Cleveland was accompanied by an illustration of the presidential grounds and glasshouses.

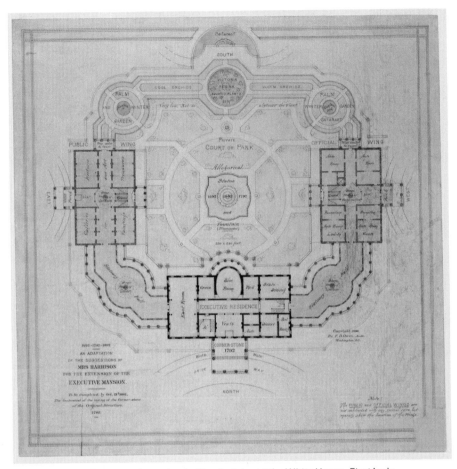

With grand ambitions and an extended family living at the White House, First Lady Caroline Harrison proposed a huge expansion project. (The "Executive Residence" on bottom of the plan is the original White House.)

Bar bets aside, the importance of this presidential trivia to the White House gardens is the middle of the Cleveland sandwich, the Harrisons. Although the White House was the largest single-family home in America from 1800 to the Civil War, by 1889 it suddenly seemed small. President Benjamin Harrison, but especially First Lady Caroline Harrison, planned changes for the White House and its gardens that moved it firmly into the Gilded Age.

Not a golden age, but a "gilded" one. Mark Twain and his gardener-writer neighbor in Hartford, Charles Dudley Warner, coined the phrase to poke fun at America's newly rich. (The phrase has a British source, namely Shakespeare's *King John*, "To gild refined gold, to paint the lily . . . is wasteful and ridiculous excess.") Ah, life before the income tax. Nineteenth-century industrialists and their offspring, who sometimes displayed more money than taste, were building vast residential establishments with gardens to match. Newport had its "cottages." George Washington Vanderbilt built more at his Biltmore in Asheville, North Carolina; James Dearing applied some of his International Harvester fortune to create a personal palazzo, the Villa Viscaya, on the shores of Biscayne Bay in Miami. Even Mark Twain ceased roughing it. As Samuel Clemens, he built a lavish domicile in Hartford, complete with gardens, greenhouses, and conservatory. Thomas Hastings, country house architect of the famed New York firm Carriere &

The extended Harrison family enjoyed the White House grounds with their pets and planted several trees. This photograph includes the president's son, Major Russell Harrison, and three grandchildren along with their goat, Old Whiskers, and one of their dogs. Benjamin Harrison was himself the grandson of President William Henry Harrison.

Hastings and a future member of the Commission of Fine Arts for the District of Columbia, advised, "The appropriation for a house should be divided into two equal parts, one-half for the house, the other for the gardens, . . . one-half for the pudding, the other for the sauce."

Mrs. Harrison's 1889 plan for the White House was generous with both pudding and sauce. The palatial design of the building tripled the size of the mansion. The plan formed a hollow square, with the existing White House as the north side, to be used as the residence. The east side would house the executive offices with a public wing to the west for gallery space, receptions, and tours. The south was reserved for plants: palm houses, lily pools, and conservatories. There was a great courtyard of filigreed flowerbeds and formal walks surrounding an allegorical fountain.

A Boston seedsman leveraged the marketing power of the White House and the First Lady to boost his sales in 1890.

Senator Leland Stanford, railroad tycoon turned politician, introduced the appropriations bill for the project from his seat as the chair of the Committee on Buildings and Grounds. But the plans were shelved. The Republicans lost control of the Senate and incoming Democrats pulled back from the lavish spending of their predecessors, the "Billion-Dollar Congress." One could almost hear future architectural historians breathe a sigh of relief.

If head gardener Henry Pfister was disappointed not to have grander greenhouses, he didn't say. By the 1893 return of Grover and Frances Cleveland, Pfister governed a collection of glasshouses from his little basement office in the southwest corner of the White House. A *New York Times* reporter described their extent, starting with the display conservatory, "undoubtedly one of the handsomest and most complete in the country, . . . filled with rare foliage and flowering plants, [it] makes a delightful annex to the White House on social occasions." To the west of the conservatory, a visitor with permission to visit the production greenhouses would walk a short distance along an asphalt walk and find a fern house, a violet house, and Grant's grapery, "a camellia house, two rose houses, two orchid houses, one propagating house, and a house for bedding plants." In the rose house alone, "several thousand rose plants are being forced, and in a short time there will be an abundance of roses of the leading varieties." One of those leading varieties was 'Catherine Mermet', a pale pink tea rose with elongated, graceful buds that was a favorite for White House table decorations.

The extensive greenhouse complex on the west side of the White House with a large set of cold frames and what appears to be a vegetable garden. On the far right is a cast-iron settee acquired during Millard Fillmore's administration at a cost of fourteen dollars from the New York firm of Janes, Beebe & Co.

A member of the horticultural staff tends the plants in the violet house at the White House.

On the slate-topped iron benches of the greenhouses were forced bulbs— narcissus, hyacinth, and lily. Florist plants included heliotrope, geranium, and cineraria, a South African plant with bright daisy-shaped flowers "larger than a silver half-dollar." Pfister continued his work with crossing and selecting amaryllis. He named a rosy-red one for Mrs. Cleveland and three others for the Cleveland daughters Ruth, Esther, and Marion. The numbers of plants under his care seem staggering. Of fuchsias alone, Pfister and his staff grew three or four hundred pots of fifty varieties, grown from cuttings each November to ensure a healthy stock.

Pfister was meticulous. His coleus were described by one visitor as "not the largest specimens I have ever seen, but they were most unquestionably the cleanest and neatest grown." He controlled the temperatures in each glasshouse. The fuchsia cuttings, for example, were kept between 45 and 55 degrees. His recipe for soil-less potting mix would still work well today. "For potting soil Mr. Pfister uses a compost consisting of two parts well rotted sod and one part rotted leaf mold with sufficient sand to lighten the soil. To an ordinary wheelbarrow full of this compost a 10-inch pot full of crushed charcoal is added with a view to keeping the soil sweet and pure."

Cineraria.

Henry Pfister watering cinerarias in the White House greenhouses.

The exterior of the display conservatory gives an indication of its size.

He did not rest on his laurels. "I have to study," Pfister once said, "in order to keep up with the times. There is a constant advance in horticultural science, and close observation is necessary to enable me to maintain my department on a par with the best foreign establishments of the kind." He was credited with an innovative and inconspicuous way of labeling plants, always an issue in gardens and greenhouses, trying to avoid that pet cemetery look. He took sturdy zinc labels and gave them, or more likely instructed his staff to give them, several coats of good white paint. When thoroughly dry, each label would get a thin coat of black paint, then the name was scratched in with a stylus, a tidy scratchboard effect.

The orchid house boasted electric lights. A self-registering thermometer with a paper dial recorded changes in temperature over a 24-hour period traced on it. One reporter noted that if the overnight staff failed to keep the boilers for the greenhouse furnace stoked, "he has an accuser which cannot be bribed."

The orchid house with its state-of-the-art technology.

Mr. P., as Pfister was sometimes called, was also responsible for the outdoor beds at the White House. In the late nineteenth century, the pendulum of horticultural style swung back to precision. Take George Washington's parterres and add masses of imported and hybridized plants, a broad palette of color, size, and shape. Stir in adequate funds, inexpensive labor, and a desire to impress. Carpet bedding is the gardening equivalent of elaborate Victorian jewelry, furniture, and fabric. It is as ornamental as the Tiffany stained glass screens and light fixtures that had adorned the interior of the White House since the 1880s.

Potted palms and agaves were hauled out of the greenhouses for a summer adorning the lawns in this gardenesque style. Pfister experimented with ornamental grasses. Crotons were popular in his bedding schemes with their bright polychrome foliage. (Related to poinsettias among others, crotons are in the euphorbia family.) Cannas joined crotons, some hybridized by Pfister himself. He christened a canna he had raised at the White House

Bigger was better as late-nineteenth-century planting beds grew taller and more elaborate.

Garden manuals such as *Henderson's Practical Floriculture* were filled with examples of paisley designs for flowerbeds.

Looking from the North Portico to Lafayette Square, one could see a catalog of the gardenesque: palms in urns and planters, ornamental conifers, patterned annual beds, and water lilies in the fountain basin.

'President Cleveland'. Enthusiasts approved of the new introduction, including one gentleman from Needham, Massachusetts, who was quoted in *Garden and Forest* magazine. Mr. Zirngiebel, "who makes a specialty of Cannas, considers President Cleveland, a salmon-scarlet, the finest bedding Canna of its color yet introduced. It is very compact, and in vividness of coloring it outshone all the others in a large patch containing sixty varieties."

Head gardener Henry Pfister submitted this photograph of pampas grass at the White House to a garden magazine in 1891.

Huge grasses, giant agaves, palms, bananas, crotons, and cannas adorned the lawns in elaborate bedding schemes. At the same time interest in old-fashioned flowers, rooted in American horticulture, did not wane. At the White House of the 1890s, behind the greenhouses, Pfister tucked a small garden with "old fashioned flowers . . . Bleeding Hearts, Columbines, Larkspurs, Irises, Spiraeas, Sweet Williams, Paeonies and other plants rich in association."

Pfister was versatile. New gardening ideas continued to make their way across the Atlantic, like some reverse Gulf Stream. William Robinson, an Irishman transplanted to England, made his name in gardening bolstered by his magazine, *The Garden*, and his many books including *The Wild Garden*. This wild side of horticulture loosed the Victorian stays of garden design by planting in relaxed drifts, then letting the plants, particularly bulbs, naturalize. It was copying nature, but also using nature. Many Americans, including Henry Pfister at the White House, took up these ideas. "No one can visit the grounds around the executive mansion at this time without being delighted with the display of bulbous plants blooming on the lawns," wrote G. W. Oliver in *Gardening* magazine. "There are crocuses and snowdrops by the thousand dotted all over some sections of the grounds without any attempt at design; they certainly look pretty."

Pfister welcomed innovation. To make lawn mowing more efficient at the White House, he brought in a horse-drawn mowing machine. Innovation was

Snowdrops gave a wild garden touch to the White House lawn.

President Cleveland opened the World's Columbian Exposition in Chicago in 1893.

about to be celebrated on a national level. On a rainy May 1, 1893, President Cleveland pressed a golden telegraph button that started the steam dynamos that powered the World's Columbian Exposition in Chicago on opening day. A capstone to the century, the Exposition commemorated, if a year late, the four hundredth anniversary of Columbus sailing the ocean blue.

The Windy City now boasted a White City, named for the Exposition's immense white Beaux Arts buildings, planned by architect Daniel Burnham. The White City sparked interest in urban planning nationwide. (It is also thought to have inspired L. Frank Baum's Emerald City in *The Wonderful Wizard of Oz*.) Frederick Law Olmsted laid out the six-hundred-acre site, transforming the swampy shore of Lake Michigan on the South Side of Chicago into what is now Jackson Park.

It was a fair of firsts, horticultural and otherwise. The Midway Plaisance, a mile-long, 220-yard-wide strip of sideshow entertainments including the "hootchy-cootchy" dances of Little Egypt, connected the fair to Washington Park to the west. (We still call these "step right up" state- and county-fairground passages "midways.") The Midway included the tallest attraction, the 264-foot Ferris wheel, a ride invented by George Washington

Gale Ferris Jr. to rival the 1889 Paris Exposition's Eiffel Tower. From the top of the wheel, riders had a bird's-eye view of the White City and Olmsted's lagoons, a naturalistic but artificial set of water features with imported Venetian gondolas and gondoliers.

The sixteen-acre Wooded Island was a picturesque jewel in the center of the main lagoon. Visitors could lose themselves in the shade of its winding paths. There was a log cabin, that quintessential symbol of the frontier settler and a part of presidential electioneering from the time of Andrew Jackson. The Japan exhibit with its traditional buildings and unusual plants attracted much attention. The island's rose garden, rhododendron beds, and flower displays inflamed plant lust and then deposited visitors at the vendor and nursery exhibits.

On the west side of the lagoon stood the great domed Horticultural Building, five acres under glass, its outdoor terraces festooned with displays of water lilies, including the giant *Victoria regia*. Those water lilies held particular interest for White House gardener Henry Pfister, who was a member of the floriculture jury specializing in aquatics as well as primulas, cinerarias, and cyclamens. He was part of an international judging panel awarding prestigious medals. Dr. Guzman came from Guatemala for the orchids, George Nicholson from England's Kew for hothouse plants, Tsuda Sen from Japan for Asian plants, and Ernest Krelage from Holland for the bulbs. Warren Manning, one of Olmsted's protégés from Massachusetts, judged the herbaceous plants. Louise Boisen from Bloomington, Indiana, judged the horticultural and botanical exhibits in the Woman's Building. (Susan B. Anthony, who made a series of speeches promoting women's suffrage at the Exposition, clearly had not yet brought equal rights to gardening.)

The Columbian Exposition planted the seeds of the Colonial Revival movement. New Jersey's State Building was a reconstruction of a "George Washington slept here" house—the Ford Mansion in Morristown—where the General had spent the winter of 1779. Its working kitchen, colonial furnishings, and costumed interpreters were simple. Charming. So different from the over-the-top Victorian styles then in vogue. It would take another ten years, but a Colonial Revival garden would eventually adorn the White House grounds.

More than twenty million visitors passed through the gates during the

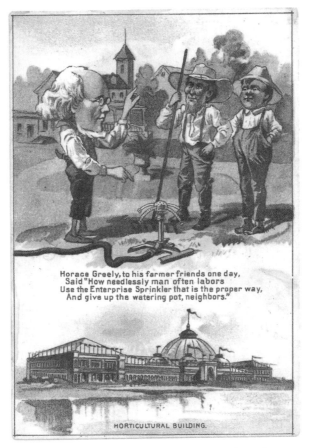

Horace Greely, to his farmer friends one day,
Said "How needlessly man often labors
Use the Enterprise Sprinkler that is the proper way,
And give up the watering pot, neighbors."

HORTICULTURAL BUILDING.

The Horticultural Building at the 1893 World's Columbian Exposition appears on this advertising card with Horace Greeley, a liberal politician who ran for president but died in 1872. It is unclear why Greeley's name was used to promote a garden sprinkler at the Chicago fair, though he was famous for his advice, "Go West, young man."

179 days of the fair, making it a tremendous driver of both culture and horticulture. "Sell the cook stove if necessary," author Hamlin Garland wrote to his father in the Dakotas, "You *must* see this fair." For gardeners, it was an extravaganza. What shopping lists the avid plant lover must have drawn up: roses, rhododendrons, and clematis from France; Lebanon cedars; silver spruces; variegated boxwood; golden English holly; and colorful cultivars of American box elder.

Thirty varieties of palms swayed around the Woman's Building, like an invitation to foreign travel. And why not? The White Star Line had its own pavilion celebrating ocean crossings via luxury steam liners. And then there was that influx of Japanese plants. So it is hardly a surprise that back at the White House that same year, 1893, Frances Cleveland planted two cut-leaf Japanese maples on the South Lawn. Perhaps it reminded her of how bands across the country had started playing "For He's Going to Marry Yum-Yum" from Gilbert and Sullivan's Japanese hit, *The Mikado*, when her engagement to Grover Cleveland was announced in 1884. John Philip Sousa, conducting the U.S. Marine Band, had played it at their wedding.

The planting bed around the South Fountain sported German irises in 1897. To the left is one of the Japanese maples planted by Frances Cleveland.

On the North Lawn, the round fountain was graced with water lilies in summer. Pfister and his staff overwintered the water lilies in brick tanks in the greenhouses. Blue water lilies from Australia joined purple from Zanzibar, red from India, and the native yellow pond lily. Across the country, parks and botanical gardens vied to have the best water garden displays. In Pittsburgh, for example, Henry Phipps donated a conservatory in 1893 that included an aquatic house stocked with plants from the World's Columbian Exposition.

Botanist Liberty Hyde Bailey proclaimed
America "the most highly favored
country in the world for the cultivation of
aquatics."

Water lilies were only one of the horticultural adornments on the North Lawn in the 1890s.

Home gardeners could also aspire to aquatics. "It seems a shame to leave any water surface in a landscape bare," *The Saturday Evening Post* admonished, "for with the help of only one or two water plants the ugliest mudhole in a meadow may be transformed into a patch of blossoming loveliness." The seeds were available from specialty suppliers, and affordable.

We don't know what the McKinleys, William and Ida, thought of the water lilies or of Cleveland's Japanese maples when they moved into the White House in 1897. They made few if any changes to the garden outdoors, and only a handful of specific demands on the conservatory. Henry Pfister, always alert to the floral favorites of a new administration, learned that First Lady Ida Saxton McKinley preferred pansies. She was often ill, beset

Ida McKinley relaxing in the conservatory, surrounded by azaleas, spider plants, and, at the top right, one of Henry Pfister's amaryllis plants.

by epilepsy, a disease essentially untreatable at the time. For White House receptions, she held a Pfister-prepared bouquet of pansies to avoid the endless shaking of visitors' hands. On quiet days her maid would lug a chair down to the center aisle of the conservatory where she could rest in a floral refuge.

President McKinley had a predilection for carnations. Pfister, not surprisingly, supplied a basket of them to the president each morning. The carnation was McKinley's signature boutonnière. It even appeared on campaign buttons for his second term, which was cut short when he was assassinated in September 1901.

After McKinley's death, the country continued to celebrate "Carnation Day" on his birthday, January 29, for many years.

Proof of the adage "a heartbeat away from the presidency," Vice President Theodore Roosevelt raised his right hand and took the oath of office. At forty-two years of age, Teddy Roosevelt was the youngest president, then and now. The former rancher, Rough Rider, New York City police commissioner, and governor of New York State moved into the White House with his substantial family. With him were Edith Kermit Carow Roosevelt and their five children—Theodore Junior, Kermit, Ethel, Archibald, and Quentin—and Alice Lee Roosevelt, the only daughter of his first marriage, whose mother had died in complications from childbirth. The place was lively but

Theodore Roosevelt Jr. and Eli in the White House conservatory. The president wrote to a young constituent, "We have a large blue macaw—Quentin calls him a polly-parrot—who lives in the greenhouse and is very friendly, but makes queer noises. He eats bread, potatoes, and coffee grains."

Archie Roosevelt salutes while his brother Quentin yawns, standing in line with the White House policemen.

bursting at the seams. Even with the children sharing bedrooms, there was barely space for a guest.

The children and their pets took over the house and gardens. Algonquin the pony was a favorite—all of the Roosevelts were great equestrians—and many photographs capture the younger children on the White House grounds atop their calico mount. Their pet macaw, Eli Yale (TR was a Harvard man), resided in the conservatory for a taste of the tropics. When the children's pet Peter Rabbit died, he was given a state funeral in the garden. Theodore Roosevelt described the scene in a letter to his older son, "Mother walked behind as chief mourner, she and Archie solemnly exchanging tributes to the worth and good qualities of the departed. Then he was buried, with a fuchsia over the little grave."

Quentin, the youngest Roosevelt, whom his mother called "a fine little bad boy," was a garden menace. He climbed the trees, sailed toy boats in the fountain, brandished the garden hose until he looked like a drowned rat,

Quentin Roosevelt and Roswell Pinckney, the son of the White House steward, take time to smell (and pick) the tulips.

"Quentee Kwee," as his father called him, up a
White House tree.

and carved a baseball diamond on the White House lawn. For winter fun, he
and his White House gang pelted the policemen stationed on the grounds
with snowballs from the roof. He once roller-skated down the newly macad-
amized drive to the pet shop on Pennsylvania Avenue. He skated back with
three snakes twined around his arms, then straight into a meeting of his
father and the attorney general. The president wrote in a letter to his son
Archie that night, "As Quentin and his menagerie were an interruption to
my interview with the Department of Justice, I suggested that he go into the
next room, where four Congressmen were drearily waiting until I should
be at leisure. I thought that he and the snakes would probably enliven their
waiting time."

The Roosevelts didn't have long to wait for a White House expansion.
They succeeded where the Harrisons had failed, employing the New York
architectural firm McKim, Mead and White. Charles McKim was in charge

of the extensive remodel—moving staircases and walls, repurposing rooms, including the staff quarters and the flower workshop. The Tiffany décor went. Paulus Hedl's anthemion railings went as well. To make room for the additions, the conservatory and greenhouses had to go.

In June 1902, *The New York Times* reported that Henry Pfister, "the German gardener who has had charge of the greenhouses and conservatories . . . is in despair to see the historic plants removed to any place where room can be found for them." Heart wrenching. To Pfister the plants were individuals. They had been loyal civil servants, decorating so many events for so many presidents. The official report from the chief of engineers is painfully blunt, "In June the United States employees in the greenhouses removed the plants therefrom, and the buildings were immediately demolished and excavation for the new building commenced." (The "new building" is the first version of what is now called the West Wing.) "Such of the old materials from the greenhouses as were worth saving were hauled to the property yards at the propagating gardens." Along with the favored few plants, including the bay trees that decorated the porticoes and terraces in summer, some of the ancillary greenhouses got a presidential pardon of sorts, as they were salvaged and re-erected at the propagating gardens near the Washington Monument.

Pfister was not so lucky. With his plants relocated, he was redundant. Henry Pfister, head gardener at the White House for thirty-five years, was dismissed in November 1902. He wasn't finished, however. In January 1903, he announced his new business at 1120 Connecticut Avenue in the District, advertising himself as "Florist and Landscape Architect." The Roosevelts gave him excellent references, including permission to use an embossed die cut of the White House on his business stationery.

George H. Brown, another landscape gardener employed by the Department of Public Buildings and Grounds, filled Pfister's White House shoes. Styles had changed. Elaborate pattern beds were *so* last century. *Country Life in America* called them "pimples on the face of nature." Even the plants came under fire, with invective hurled at the "stereotyped beds," the "prim rows" of cannas and sheared coleus, the hyacinths and tulips, and the "screaming scarlet geraniums." It was time for a change.

Thus in 1903, when President Roosevelt and his family retreated from Washington to Oyster Bay for the summer, Brown installed a new garden

TELEPHONE MAIN 3495

Henry Pfister

FLORIST & LANDSCAPE ARCHITECT

LATE IN CHARGE OF THE WHITE HOUSE
CONSERVATORIES AND GROUNDS.

1120 CONNECTICUT AVENUE.

Washington, D.C. Jan 27 1903

Mr. _____

_____

Mr. Henry Pfister who, for the past twenty-five years has had direct charge of all the floral decorations of the White House on all State and other occasions, has opened a Florist Store at 1120 Connecticut Avenue, and invites the honor of your patronage.

He is prepared to execute promptly all orders for cut flowers, floral designs and plants.

In addition to supplying cut flowers, plants, etc., of all descriptions, he will personally design and provide floral decorations for Receptions, Dinners, Weddings and other functions, in the latest and most approved style.

Having had long experience in the Art of Landscaping in Paris, London, and in different sections of this country, he will make Landscape-Gardening a specialty; will furnish plans and estimates for the laying out, altering and planting of grounds; will contract for the proper supervision and keeping in order of private gardens and grounds.

Mr. Pfister's long experience in Landscape-Gardening enables him to guarantee his patrons the most effective and permanent results.   Yours respectfully,

Henry Pfister

My dear Mr. Clarke

Your kind offer of last Sunday is accepted for to morrow evening.

Come out early & take dinner with us after dinner we can start on the Envelopes

The Circulars are not yet ready, this is the first print without the embossed White House, the die not being yet ready the circulars will not be ready before friday or Sat.

Yours very truly Henry Pfister

Jan. 27. 1903.

Henry Pfister's letter announcing his new business.

on the south side of the White House. Just as McKim, Mead and White designed Colonial Revival treatments for the interior, Brown provided a Colonial Revival garden for the exterior. It still had tidy beds, oval and vaguely vase-shaped, but they were loosely filled with old-fashioned plants. *The Washington Post* commented: "Landscape gardeners have noticed the tendency to return to colonial flowers to harmonize with the colonial style of architecture which has become so popular. When our ancestors were constructing their houses with stately columns they were fond of ornamenting their lawns with plants and flowers of the woods, obtained at little cost and expenditure of energy. . . . Conspicuous among the new White House flora will be the golden rod. What has been termed 'old-fashioned' flowers will be given places of honor in the new gardens because of their beauty and hardy nature."

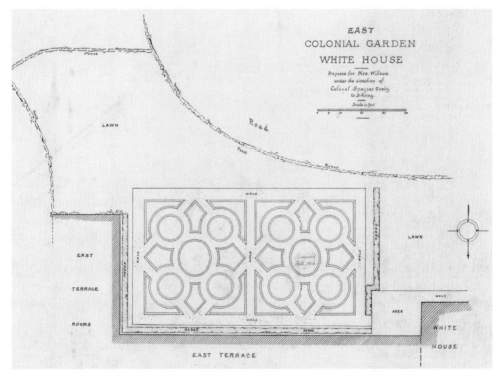

The geometric outlines of the Roosevelts' colonial gardens harken back to George Washington's Mount Vernon. In this later plan, they were redrawn for Ellen Wilson who had them removed.

Roses, pansies, daisies, and other old-fashioned flowers fill the box-lined
Colonial Revival beds in 1902.

Perhaps Brown or one of the Roosevelts had read the new and popular
book in praise of colonial gardens by Alice Morse Earle. Published in 1902,
Old Time Gardens was one of the first gardening books illustrated with pho-
tography throughout. Earle included photographs of Mount Vernon's boxwood parterres and a tantalizing but indistinct (and further undescribed)
image of "The Garden of Abigail Adams." Her topics included "Box Edg-
ings," "Old Flower Favorites," and "Roses of Yesterday." The White House
garden was edged in boxwood and its beds planted with annuals, perennials,
and flowering shrubs. Roses filled the center beds and climbing roses with
clematis clambered up alongside the president's new offices.

The Roosevelts looked on what they had created and were pleased. They
enjoyed the view of the Jackson magnolia, in bloom or out, near their bedroom window. Theodore Roosevelt came close to being "bully on flowers."
One May evening, Roosevelt wrote to his eldest son, Ted: "I think I get more

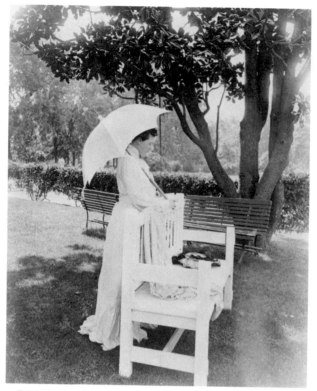

Edith Roosevelt in the White House garden.

fond of flowers every year. The grounds are now at that high stage of beauty in which they will stay for the next two months." He described the spring flowers, bright in the cool sunshine at the White House. "The buckeyes are in bloom, the pink dogwood, and the fragrant lilacs, which are almost the loveliest of the bushes; and then the flowers, including the lily-of-the-valley."

Edith Roosevelt had photographs taken and her portrait painted on the white wooden bench near the flowerbeds. Her husband took to calling the space "Mother's garden." He told Ted, "I do not think that any two people ever got more enjoyment out of the White House than Mother and I. We love the house itself, without and within, for its associations, for its stillness and its simplicity. We love the garden. And we like Washington. We almost always take our breakfast on the south portico now, Mother looking very pretty and dainty in her summer dresses."

Dreer's Specialties in Seeds, Plants and Bulbs

We give below a mere hint of the many new and rare things we have to offer this season. All are faithfully described and many illustrated in our **Garden Book for 1906**, acknowledged to be the best, most complete and comprehensive catalogue of gardening needs ever published. A copy will be sent Free if you mention this magazine.

FIVE NEW VEGETABLES

Early Model Beet. A beautiful globe shape variety, rich blood red and matures very early. Pkt.; 10 cts.; oz., 15 cts.; ¼ lb., 40 cts., postpaid.
Dreer's Aristocrat Sugar Corn. The sweetest of all. Ears large and mature early. Pkt., 10 cts.; pt., 30 cts.; qt., 50 cts., postpaid.
May King Lettuce. Heads delightfully crisp and tender; quick growth good for forcing or open ground. Pkt., 10 cts.; oz., 30 cts.; ¼ lb., $1.00, postpaid.
The Harbinger Pea. An English variety which is very dwarf, but produces large pods in abundance. Peas are very tender and sweet. Pkt., 10 cts.; pt., 33 cts.; qt., 55 cts., postpaid.
Dreer's Earliest Cluster Tomato. The earliest and best extra early variety. Produces fruits in immense clusters and the quality is excellent. Pkt., 15c.; ½ oz., 30 cts.; oz., 50 cts.; ¼ lb., $1.50, postpaid.
We will send postpaid one packet each of the above five grand vegetables for 40 cts.

NEW FLOWER SEEDS

New Aster, White Fleece.
Among the many new things in Flower Seeds this season may be mentioned:
Aster White Fleece. A plumey globe of snow white. 20 cts. per pkt.
Aster Violet King. A fine shade of clear violet. 25 cts. pkt.
Calliopsis Golden Ray. Quaint and pretty gold and brown flowers. 15 cts. per pkt.
Coreopsis Golden Fleece. A double flowering type of this popular hardy flower. 25 cts. per pkt.
Delphinium Gold Medal Hybrids. The very finest of the hardy Larkspurs. 25 cts. per pkt.
Nicotiana Sanderae Hybrids. 8 new colors of this glorious new annual. 25c per collection.
Salpiglossis. A fine set of this charming annual; 6 colors, 40 cts. per set.
Sweet Peas, Orchid and Gloxinia flowered, the latest and best of all. 6 colors, $1.00 per set.

NOVELTIES IN PLANTS AND BULBS

New Cactus Dahlia, General Buller.
New Calla, Mrs. Roosevelt. Superb sort, 50 cts. each.
New Ageratum, Inimitable. The largest and finest to date. 25 cts. each.
Five Superb New Gladiolus. $1.25 for the set.
Delphinium Belladonna, the ever-blooming turquoise blue hardy Larkspur. 25 cts. each.
Three New Shasta Daisies. 50 cts. for the 3.
In **Dahlias** we offer 29 new double sorts, mostly of the Cactus type, but including Decorative, Show and Fancy sorts. The entire set for $10.00.
Five New Century Single Dahlias for $3.00.
Five Grand New Single Dahlias of the regular type for $1.75.
New Roses, New Geraniums, New Phloxes, etc., etc.

All of the above and hundreds of others are described and illustrated in our .. **GARDEN BOOK FOR 1906** which will be sent FREE on application. Please mention this magazine.

HENRY A. DREER, - 714 Chestnut Street, Philadelphia, Pa.

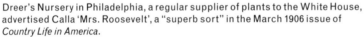

Dreer's Nursery in Philadelphia, a regular supplier of plants to the White House, advertised Calla 'Mrs. Roosevelt', a "superb sort" in the March 1906 issue of *Country Life in America.*

Striped awnings that jutted out between the columns of the South Portico shaded their breakfast. It would have been especially inviting in late May. Roosevelt continued, "There are plenty of flowers in bloom or just coming out, the honeysuckle most conspicuously. The south portico is fragrant with that now. The jasmine will be out later."

The flowering vines that twined up the White House railing were mirrored at houses large and small across the country, an adornment anyone could afford. One gardening manual of the period stated unequivocally, "Your homes may lack the paint, gilding and tapestry that adorn those of your neighbors, but if vines are trained over the doors and windows, they will present a fresh beauty and glory every Summer's morn which the products of art cannot surpass." The best things in life are almost free.

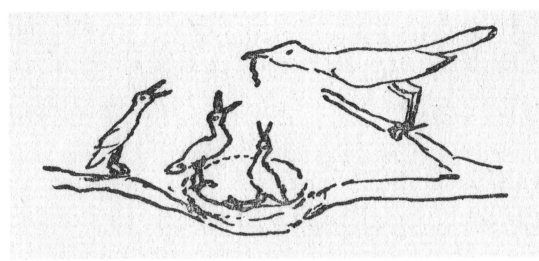

Teddy Roosevelt, a dedicated bird watcher, sent this drawing in a letter from the White House to Quentin in June 1904, reporting "the little birds in the nest in the vines on the garden fence are nearly grown up."

Picture "Mother" in her summer dress on the arm of the president, walking down the steps of the South Portico with its scented railings. They had a regular routine, as Teddy Roosevelt reported to his son Kermit: "We stroll about the garden for fifteen or twenty minutes, looking at the flowers and the fountain and the trees. Then I work until between four and five, usually having some official people to lunch—now a couple of Senators, now a couple of Ambassadors, now a literary man, now a capitalist or a labor leader, or a scientist, or a big-game hunter. If Mother wants to ride, we then spend a couple of hours on horseback . . . If we don't ride I walk or play tennis."

Tennis anyone? The American backyard was becoming a magnet for sports and fitness. With improved transportation and ice-cooled refrigerator railroad cars to transport vegetables and fruits from truck farms, less space was needed for orchard and kitchen gardens, leaving more space for recreation. Food gardening at the White House gradually disappeared, leaving only a bed of mint cultivated for tea and desserts. For Teddy Roosevelt, the White House grounds got their first permanent recreational facility. A tennis court was built adjacent to the temporary executive offices, as the West Wing was first called. Roosevelt's team was quickly dubbed the "Tennis Cabinet."

The Roosevelts used the South Lawn for receptions as well as tennis. On the left, the Marine Band is playing.

President Theodore Roosevelt's contributions to the conservation of nature and the landscape are legion. He created more than fifty bird sanctuaries. (Roosevelt once sent a list of ninety-three birds he had observed in and around the White House to a local author who was revising *Birds of Washington and Vicinity*.) During his administration, Congress established five national parks and the National Forest Service. A Conservation Commission prepared the first inventory of the country's natural resources. Using a provision in the Antiquities Act of 1906, he flexed his executive muscle and designated 150 national forests and 18 national monuments, Muir Woods and the Grand Canyon among them. By the end of his second term in 1909, he could take credit for preserving 230,000,000 acres of land.

Between concern for the White House grounds and the national wilderness, Teddy Roosevelt also had a hand in a major change to the District of Columbia. He threw his support behind the McMillan Plan, named for James McMillan, senator from Michigan who sponsored a study of the District's parks and public spaces. The Senate appointed architect Charles McKim, already in town for his White House project, to the commission. A second architect, Daniel Burnham of World's Columbian Exposition fame, joined him, as did landscape architect Frederick Law Olmsted Jr. Sculptor Augustus Saint-Gaudens completed the group. Just as Theodore Roosevelt, with McKim's help, had rid the White House of its Victoriana, the Commission's sweeping proposals for the National Mall and the monumental core of the city undid most of the winding designs of Andrew Jackson Downing and incursions such as Central Market and the tracks and terminal of the B&O Railroad. Vistas would be restored, allées planted, and a new memorial to Lincoln built as a counterweight to the Capitol on the west end of the Mall. It was a return to formality, and America's urban planners took it up with gusto. They called the movement "City Beautiful." Peter L'Enfant would have approved.

Home Front

∾

Can Vegetables, Fruit, and the Kaiser Too.

NATIONAL WAR GARDENS COMMISSION, 1918

Urban Washington with the propagating greenhouses near the Washington Monument and the grown-in executive grounds stretching from Lafayette Square to the Tidal Basin.

TON

THE NATION

1910S–1940S

(1909–1913) WILLIAM AND HELEN TAFT

(1913–1921) WOODROW AND ELLEN WILSON (DIED 1914),
THEN EDITH WILSON (MARRIED 1915)

(1921–1923) WARREN AND FLORENCE HARDING

(1923–1929) CALVIN AND GRACE COOLIDGE

(1929–1933) HERBERT AND LOU HOOVER

(1933–1945) FRANKLIN AND ELEANOR ROOSEVELT

W ILLIAM HOWARD TAFT motored into the presidency in 1909, adding the first automobiles to the executive transportation fleet. The October prior, just before Taft won the election, Model-T number one rolled out of Henry Ford's Detroit factory. The automobile was poised to change the landscape of America.

Taft was a famously large man, mustached and affable. His chauffeur described the president settling into the backseat of his automobile to watch the trees whiz by. Taft called the feeling thus induced "atmospheric champagne." The car matched the man. Taft's 1909 White Steam Car was a behemoth of a machine, built by White's Sewing Machine Company in his home state of Ohio. Two gasoline-powered Pierce-Arrows completed the executive automotive acquisitions, and in the White House stables some of the feed bins gave way to gas pumps.

Despite his appreciation of motor transport, Taft chose the more familiar horse-drawn over a horseless carriage for the inauguration on March 4, 1909. Perhaps it was tradition. Perhaps it was the weather. The wind howled, and hundreds of men worked to clear the morning's ten-inch snowfall from the parade route that day. For the first time in presidential history, the first lady, Helen Taft, joined her husband in the carriage after the swearing in for the official ride from the Capitol to the White House.

Helen "Nellie" Taft was a go-getter. She had always wanted to be in the

Horse-drawn and motorized vehicles join pedestrians in front of 1600 Pennsylvania Avenue. Hyacinths fill a bed in Lafayette Park and magnolias bloom on the North Lawn across the street.

William and Helen Taft were an experienced and well-traveled team when they arrived at the White House in 1909.

White House, though her ambitions, understandable given the era, extended only to presidential spouse. She was a progressive who supported public kindergartens, workplace reform, and, eventually, women's suffrage. For the White House gardens, she wanted to brighten things up, and gardener George Brown obliged, planting "pansies, marguerites, geraniums (four colors) and begonias (two colors)." Brown's superior wrote that Taft was "anxious to have the work done as soon as possible after to-day, so that the gardens will present an attractive appearance for the Garden Party next Friday." No doubt Brown planted "promptly and artistically" on behalf of the new first lady during that first week of May 1909. While Brown was dutifully setting out the annuals for her fête, Helen Taft was setting off on a project that would leave a perennial mark on the national landscape, not with garden parties, but with cherry trees.

While the saying goes "American as apple pie," there is something about the cherry. In elementary school until recent years, American children

President Taft, standing center, examines a lilac bloom with a guest while the first lady, seated at left, looks on. Lilacs, presumably cut on the grounds, fill a tall glass vase on the table with the punch bowl. On the far left stands Major Archibald Butt, White House military attaché, who drowned in 1912 on the Titanic along with his companion, artist Francis Davis Millet.

learned that young George Washington could not tell a lie to his father about having chopped down the cherry tree. While this turns out to be a tale fabricated by Washington's earliest biographer, Parson Weems, to explicate the childhood character of our first president, it has made its way into the national consciousness. But if cherry tree removal is connected to the father of our country, cherry tree installation in Washington and in public spaces around America had two mothers and a father: Eliza Scidmore, Helen Taft, and David Fairchild.

This period postcard evokes the tall tale of young George Washington.

If you happened to be the superintendent of the Office of Public Buildings and Grounds, Eliza Scidmore (pronounced SID-more) was something of a pest. She was a woman on a mission, a quest that had already stretched out for years. This unpaid but determined garden lobbyist wanted, for Washington D.C., a display of cherry blossoms to match the ones she had seen in Tokyo as a young woman.

Scidmore did not lack credentials. After studying at Oberlin for two years and learning the journalistic ropes, she was bitten by the travel bug. Travel she did, from Asia to Alaska. She wrote lively travel books. She became a reporter-photographer for the National Geographic Society, and she was the first woman elected to its board of managers. Of all the places she had visited, Japan held her heart. In her popular book *Jinrikisha Days in Japan*, she captured Tokyo thawing into spring: "A fortnight, a month of melting snows, cold rains, and dull skies, and lo! The branches of the withered, old black plum-trees are starred with fragrant white flowers. For a few days a hazy calm hushes the air, sounds are veiled, light is softened, and spring has really come, no matter how many sullen relapses it may suffer before the glorious April cloud-burst of cherry blossoms decks the empire in wreaths of white and pink, and fills the people with joy." This vision of petals, the "sakura" beloved of the Japanese, became Eliza Scidmore's ambition for Washington D.C.

Just as Frances Cleveland had planted Japanese maples at the White House, Americans had a continued enthusiasm for horticultural *Japonisme*. In 1906, Charles Pfizer, son of the pharmaceutical company founder, installed a three-and-a-half-acre Japanese garden on his estate in Bernardsville, New Jersey, with the help of a Japanese gardener, a Mr. K. Takahashi, and a Japanese carpenter. The only other necessary ingredients were "patience and a generous money allowance." Pfizer had plenty of the latter, and he seems to have had the patience too, at least based on the name of his estate. It was named "Yademos," or "Someday" spelled backward. Alas, the cherry trees he imported for the garden at Yademos did not thrive.

David Fairchild had more success. A veteran plant explorer and head of the United States Department of Agriculture's Office of Seed and Plant Introductions, Fairchild entitled his memoir *The World Was My Garden*. He wasn't exaggerating. Like Scidmore, this world traveler had been taken with the people and plants of Japan. "Fairy," as his friends knew him, imported 125 cherry trees from the Yokohama Nursery Company for his Maryland home in 1905. When they proved hardy, he bought more and distributed them to schoolchildren for a 1908 Arbor Day planting around Washington. He invited Eliza Scidmore to a lecture that capped the festivities and seconded her idea of a major planting around Potomac Park.

The following spring, Scidmore wrote to enlist the support of First Lady Helen Taft for the project. What a warm wave of satisfaction she must have felt when she opened this reply:

> The White House, Washington
> April 7, 1909
> Thank you very much for your suggestion about the cherry trees. I have taken the matter up and am promised the trees, but I thought perhaps it would be best to make an avenue of them, extending down to the turn in the road, as the other part is still too rough to do any planting. Of course, they could not reflect in the water, but the effect would be very lovely of the long avenue. Let me know what you think about this.
> Sincerely yours,
> Helen H. Taft

Taft could envision a sweep of flowering cherry trees along the Tidal Basin in Potomac Park, reclaimed land south of the White House built by the Army Corps of Engineers as a flood control project in the 1880s. The park was perfect. It already had a road, just right for the presidential automobiles, though under her influence the "Speedway" was rechristened to the more sedate "Potomac Drive." The Tidal Basin at the heart of the park would provide a central water feature. Workers could erect a bandstand. The tree planting would enhance the vista from the White House, complementing the Washington Monument. In the park, she could recreate one of her favorite public spaces, Manila's Luneta.

In the aftermath of the Spanish-American War, Teddy Roosevelt had appointed William Howard Taft the governor-general of the Philippines. From 1901 through 1903 the Tafts had relished their life at the sumptuous Malacañang Palace, now perhaps better known for housing Imelda Marcos and her shoe collection. Taft also brought Daniel Burnham to Manila. This architect of Chicago's World's Columbian Exposition, New York's Flatiron Building, and Washington's Union Station, created a city plan for Manila that included Helen Taft's fondly remembered Luneta Park. She had memories of carriage rides along its waterfront drive, listening to the military bands in the cool of summer evenings, and strolling its fashionable esplanade.

With Manila in mind, the first lady was "determined, if possible, to convert Potomac Park into a glorified Luneta where all Washington could meet, either on foot or in vehicles, at five o'clock on certain evenings, listen to band concerts and enjoy such recreation as no other spot in Washington could possibly afford." It was to be democracy dressed as a park, filled with the music that she loved, under the bloom of Japanese flowering cherries.

Helen Taft accepted a donation of two thousand trees from the mayor of Tokyo as a gift from the people of Japan. But the shipment of Tokyo trees was a disaster. It arrived in 1910 so badly infested with pests and disease that David Fairchild wrote, "I found myself in a hornets' nest of protesting pathologists and entomologists." The trees were burned, and with them the project might have gone up in smoke.

With a combination of deft public relations and diplomacy, Fairchild kept the project alive, though, like Charles Pfizer's Yademos, it would require

Scidmore, Fairchild, and Taft were right. The Tidal Basin cherry trees drew visitors from the start.

patience. Gardeners in Japan selected fresh cuttings from the famous collection along the Arakawa River in suburban Tokyo and grafted them onto healthy rootstock grown in Hyogo Prefecture. On a March day in 1912, the SS *Awa Maru* docked in Seattle with a cargo of some six thousand young and healthy saplings. The trees were transferred to insulated boxcars. Half were sent to New York, where some still bloom around the Central Park Reservoir. The other half, 3,020 to be precise, arrived in Washington on March 26. There were twelve different varieties; the majority were Yoshino.

The next day, March 27, 1912, Helen Taft and the wife of the Japanese ambassador, the Viscountess Chinda, planted the first two trees on the north edge of the Tidal Basin. Afterward Taft gave the Viscountess a bouquet of 'American Beauty' roses. Eliza Scidmore attended the ceremony. Then the men of the Department of Public Buildings and Grounds got busy planting. In addition to the Tidal Basin, they planted twenty specimens of the green-flowered 'Gyoiko' around the fountain on the South Lawn of the White House. As David Fairchild put it, "I never dared to imagine the popular enthusiasm which these Washington trees have caused throughout the country." The Cherry Blossom Festival is still a heavily attended annual event in Washington D. C., and festivals bloom nationwide from San Francisco to Brooklyn, from Denver to Macon, Georgia, and more.

During the Taft administration, the Oval Office was added to the West Wing, nudging Teddy Roosevelt's tennis court farther out on the South Lawn. The lawn was getting national attention, with individuals and institutions starting to buy specialty grass seed to create fine turf. In 1912 Michell's of Philadelphia advertised its grass seed as "Ready for Mowing 4 to 5 Weeks from Sowing" including "On the White House Grounds at Washington, at all recent National and International Expositions . . . in the best known public parks, and finest estates." From the windows of the White House, the president would sometimes catch a glimpse of Pauline Wayne, a Holstein cow whose domestic duties included producing fresh milk and butter for the Taft table. A gift of Senator Isaac Stephenson of Wisconsin, Pauline was the last cow to graze and fertilize the White House lawn.

With the automobile in ascension, stables and barnyards were retreating at residential properties throughout the country. The garage and the driveway were taking their places. White House workers converted the stable

HENDERSON'S CLIMBING AMERICAN BEAUTY ROSE— SEE PAGE 153

1930

EVERYTHING FOR THE GARDEN
PETER HENDERSON & CO
35 & 37 CORTLANDT ST., NEW YORK

The 'American Beauty' rose, named and popularized by George Field, a Washington D.C. nurseryman who previously had been White House head gardener, was followed by new introductions such as 'Climbing American Beauty' that cashed in on the name.

Pauline Wayne, the last White House cow. (The Second Empire building in the background is just west of the White House and housed the State, War, and Navy Departments. Today it is known as the Eisenhower Executive Office Building.)

The old-fashioned garden is front and center in this spoof of Taft, who seemed old line compared to his progressive predecessor Teddy Roosevelt.

to accommodate the Tafts' new vehicles. In time, the horses, cow, carriages, and cars were moved off the White House grounds entirely.

In the broader landscape, the nation's emerging love affair with the automobile expanded into scenic drives. In Washington, as in other developing urban areas, parkways were connecting downtowns to growing bedroom communities, with residents who slept in one place and worked in another. Congress authorized the development of Rock Creek and Potomac Parkway in 1913. Once built it would take motorists on a picturesque route from Potomac Park through Rock Creek Park to suburban Maryland. The same route that John Quincy Adams used to walk and Theodore and Edith Roosevelt used to traverse on horseback would now be open to a new generation of motorists, presidential and otherwise.

Like fashions or political power, some gardens rise and fall quickly. Others persist. Edith Roosevelt's colonial garden, planted in 1903, was enjoyed by the Roosevelts and the Tafts during its ten-year run but was about to be supplanted. A new first lady, Ellen Axson Wilson, had a new idea in mind.

In July 1913, at Wilson's request, one Beatrix Jones sent a letter to Colonel Spencer Cosby, the engineer responsible for the White House, at the Office of Public Buildings and Grounds. It was typed on Jones's embossed stationery announcing her profession, "Landscape Gardener," her address "21 East Eleventh Street New York," and her cable address "BEAVRY." Enclosed were working drawings for the East Garden of the White House. Several days before, a handwritten note from Wilson's secretary, Helen Woodrow Bones, had alerted Colonel Cosby to the plan's imminent arrival. "Mrs. Wilson thinks you will be pleased with Miss Jones's scheme," penned Bones encouragingly.

Jones's plan, inked on fabric at one-eighth-inch scale and hand colored, was Italianate. Simple and symmetrical, its box borders, gravel path, and evergreen hedge enclosed a rectangular reflecting pool with marble coping. It was allied with the architecture of the White House, an outdoor room for elegant entertaining.

It isn't surprising that Jones designed a garden like this. She had studied with family friend Charles Sprague Sargent and his staff at the Arnold Arboretum, learning "to make the plan fit the ground and not twist the ground to fit the plan." After that she, like so many of her social class, had taken the Grand Tour, studying gardens of Italy and France, Germany and England.

Ellen Wilson was adept at art and garden making. While her husband was president of Princeton University, she created a new garden for their residence at Prospect House, then rendered it in oils.

Her favorite aunt, author Edith Wharton, had written a popular book called *Italian Villas and their Gardens*, published in 1904.

It isn't surprising that Ellen Wilson would want an Italianate garden, summering, as the Wilsons did, in a Cornish, New Hampshire, house designed by architect Charles Platt. Platt's book, *Italian Gardens*, was distilled from his own travels in Italy in the 1890s. It would have been reasonable for Wilson to hire him for the White House gardens, as he also handled landscapes for his clients, including many around garden-rich Cornish. But for some reason, Beatrix Jones got the nod. Perhaps Wilson remembered her from Princeton. The two women had met at Prospect House while Woodrow Wilson was president of the university from 1902 through 1910. Or perhaps Ellen Wilson, an artist in her own right, simply wanted Jones, the only woman among the founding members of the American Society of Landscape Architects, to have the commission.

It also isn't surprising that Colonel Cosby was less than thrilled with Beatrix Jones. His Office of Public Buildings and Grounds had its own landscape architect, thank you very much, the MIT-trained George Burnap. Burnap, experienced in park design, had created a sedate Italianate rose garden, ornamented with trellising and a statue of the god Pan, to flank the West Wing. It was installed without much fanfare in the fall of 1913. The White House grounds had long been under the aegis of the Army Corps of Engineers, in the War Department. The Colonel was an officer in the United States Army, first in his class at West Point, and unaccustomed, one supposes, to dealing with professional women.

Horace W. Peaslee, an associate of George Burnap, drew this preliminary sketch for Mrs. Wilson's rose garden. The lattice created temporary gallery space to display her paintings at garden parties and hid a drying yard with clotheslines.

When, two months later, a seven-page plant list from Jones arrived on Colonel Cosby's desk, one can only imagine his reaction. Rather than a simple evergreen border with a central pool, the list overflows with peonies, bulbs, roses, hollyhocks, bleeding heart, irises. Actually Jones used the botanical names: *Paeonia*, *Narcissus*, *Rosa*, and so on. Perhaps she thought that proper nomenclature was expected; it certainly had been during her time at the Arnold Arboretum. To Cosby, it probably seemed pretentious.

The Wilsons' West Garden with the President's Walk, edged with rose standards, bordering the West Wing.

A statue of Pan, a popular subject for early-twentieth-century garden sculpture, played on his pipes in the White House garden until the 1940s.

Pan appeared among the tulips on the program cover for the 1933 International Flower Show, held in New York's Grand Central Palace.

Beatrix Jones's watercolor rendering of the East Garden.

It was a case of Italianate meets English. In England, Beatrix Jones had met Gertrude Jekyll, the doyenne of the English perennial border, and befriended William Robinson, the aforementioned garden editor-writer and promoter of the "wild garden." Jones helped introduce these new planting styles to her clientele across the pond, a roster of society names including Whitney, Morgan, and Rockefeller. Her planting plan for the White House East Garden was flowing and saturated with color, much like the impressionistic canvases painted by Ellen Wilson. (Wilson had excelled in oils in

classes at New York's Art Students' League before her marriage, and later in the studios of Old Lyme, Connecticut.) Jones's planting plan was the latest thing—appropriate for a lady, especially a first lady.

When she posted her plant list to Washington, Beatrix Jones was physically in Great Britain. The fact that the list had a cover letter addressed from a Scottish hunting lodge—Jones regularly spent summers there as hostess for one of her golf-playing bachelor cousins—must have added bitterness to Colonel Cosby's pill. Jones, we might add, projected an attitude. "I cannot urge too strongly the necessity of buying the very best Stock possible," she wrote, "as I think we are agreed that the place being so conspicuous, should either be done well or not at all." As if the Colonel needed coaching.

Gardening, like many human endeavors, breeds possessiveness. By mid-September it was clear that Colonel Cosby had spoken with the first lady about the plan and gotten the upper hand. Mrs. Wilson's secretary confirmed the agreement in writing, "The original plan is to be modified so that in many instances material on hand may be used in place of things suggested by Miss Jones." A subsequent letter from Cosby's office informed Jones of the changes. "We shall be able to adhere to your plans without going to the expense necessary to purchase new material." In other words, the plants would come from whatever was available at the government propagating grounds. He emphasized, "This course was adopted only after consultation with Mrs. Wilson."

Work got started in September 1913. The head gardener marked out the ground using the base map drawn by Beatrix Jones. Heavy clay was hauled out—177 wagonloads—and amended topsoil hauled in. Masons poured the concrete basin for the pool and set the marble coping. Gardeners planted new hedges of privet and boxwood. But for various reasons, the garden remained unfinished. Weddings were a distraction. Two of the Wilson daughters were married at the White House in close succession, Jessie in November 1913 in the East Room and Nell in May 1914 in the Blue. Then the distractions darkened. Ellen Axson Wilson fell ill and died in the White House, succumbing to Bright's disease in August of that year.

The garden that Jones designed and Cosby altered would have to wait for a third Wilson wedding. In March 1915, Woodrow Wilson's cousin introduced him to Edith Bolling Galt, a widow with smiling violet eyes and stylish attire. "You are the only woman I know who can wear an orchid," Wilson told her, "On everybody else, the orchid wears the woman." Though Wilson seemed, as one commentator put it, "more Apothecary than Romeo," their relationship grew, and they married six months later at Galt's home at 1308 20th Street N.W., near Dupont Circle.

It was Edith Wilson who revived the plans for the East Garden, negotiating the shoals between Colonel Cosby and the first Mrs. Wilson's chosen landscape architect. In January 1916 Beatrix Jones Farrand—by this time,

While new gardens were being made south of the White House, on the north side gardeners continued with displays of tropical plants like cannas, as shown on the back cover of the 1914 Conard and Jones catalog. (The swastika in this pre–Nazi era publication was an innocent indicator of new plant introductions.)

Jones had met and married Yale historian Max Farrand—sent a new, limited plant list. It avoids the botanical nomenclature, but still includes her signature specifics: "For early spring flower there should be three or four hundred bulbs of Crocus Mont Blanc or Giant Yellow, planted irregularly in the grass. These had better be sown or scattered from a basket, as if they are placed by hand, they will inevitably be planted in close little groups, whereas they should appear to grow in groups of natural shape in the grass." For later spring, Darwin tulips followed—pink 'Clara Butt' and cerise 'Pride

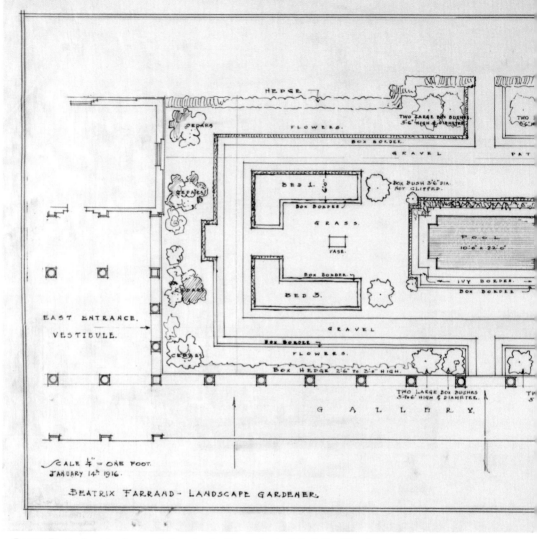

Beatrix Farrand's revised presentation plan for the garden installed after Woodrow Wilson's marriage to Edith Bolling Galt.

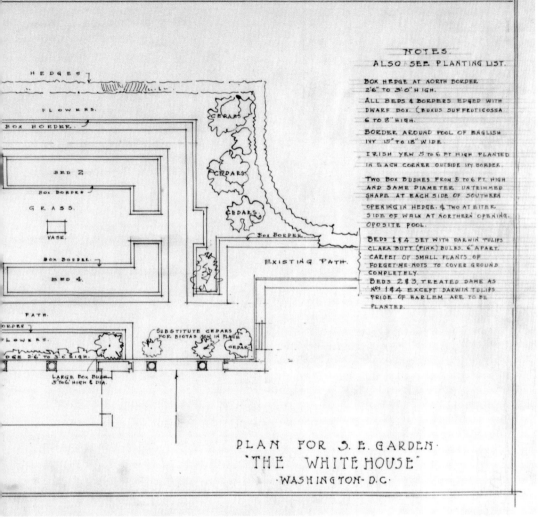

NOTES.
ALSO SEE PLANTING LIST.

BOX HEDGE AT NORTH BORDER
2'6" TO 3'0" HIGH.

ALL BEDS & BORDERS EDGED WITH
DWARF BOX. (BUXUS SUFFRUTICOSSA
6 TO 8" HIGH.

BORDER AROUND POOL OF ENGLISH
IVY 15" TO 18" WIDE.

IRISH YEW 5 TO 6 FT HIGH PLANTED
IN EACH CORNER OUTSIDE IVY BORDER.

TWO BOX BUSHES FROM 5 TO 6 FT. HIGH
AND SAME DIAMETER UNTRIMMED
SHAPE AT EACH SIDE OF SOUTHERN
OPENING IN HEDGE. & TWO AT EITHER
SIDE OF WALK AT NORTHERN OPENING.
OPOSITE POOL.

BEDS 1 & 4 SET WITH DARWIN TULIPS
CLARA BUTT (PINK) BULBS. 6" APART.
CARPET OF SMALL PLANTS OF
FORGET-ME-NOTS TO COVER GROUND
COMPLETELY.
BEDS 2 & 3 TREATED SAME AS
Nos 1 & 4 EXCEPT DARWIN TULIPS
PRIDE OF HARLEM ARE TO BE
PLANTED.

HEDGES

FLOWERS.

BOX BORDER.

CEDARS

CEDARS

CEDARS

BED 2

BOX BORDER

GRASS.

VASE.

BOX BORDER

BED 4.

BOX BORDER

EXISTING PATH.

PATH.

BORDER
FLOWERS.
DGER 2'6" TO 3'0" HIGH.

LARGE BOX BUSH.
5' TO 6' HIGH & DIA.

SUBSTITUTE CEDARS
FOR BIOTAS NOW IN PLACE

CEDAR

PLAN FOR S. E. GARDEN.
"THE WHITE HOUSE"
·WASHINGTON· D.C.

Edith and Woodrow Wilson enjoy the East Garden in their summer finery.

of Haarlem'—interspersed with blue forget-me-nots. Then heliotropes for summer, when the tulips "grow shabby." Farrand's finale was a display of chrysanthemums, gold and deep maroon, "for late autumn effect."

The garden was at last finished in 1916. It appears that Colonel Cosby or the gardener, George Brown, pocket-vetoed some of Mrs. Farrand's directives. Photographs tell the tale. Water lilies bloomed in the pool, a pool surrounded by irises instead of tulips. Still, Farrand's design footprint was there, and the garden was lovely. The president and new first lady stood smiling for the photographer, he in his boater, blazer, and white bucks; she with her signature orchid and one of her elaborate summer hats, millinery that rivals the blooms.

The following April, America entered World War I. Garden projects took a backseat as the workforce was diverted to defense. By the spring of 1918, a herd of twenty Hampshire sheep took up residence on the South Lawn of the

Sheep safely graze the White House lawn during World War I, keeping the grass short when workers were hard to find.

White House to keep the grass closely cropped. It was a visible sign of support when so many of the boys were "Over There." Wool was in high demand, and the wool shorn from the White House sheep was auctioned as a novelty item to benefit the American Red Cross. *The Ladies' Home Journal* reported that for the ninety-eight pounds of wool, the proceeds were $52,828.

The federal government, through the National War Garden Commission, touted growing and preserving food at home. The members of the Garden Club of America, founded in 1913, and the Woman's National Farm and Garden Association, founded by three Bryn Mawr alumnae in 1914, threw their energies into teaching horticulture and raising money for the Red Cross. Henrietta Stout, a dahlia expert and founding member of the "Nine of Spades" Garden Club of Short Hills, New Jersey, sold tubers of her 'Sunshine' hybrid with all receipts directed to war work. Gardening schools, such as the Pennsylvania School of Horticulture for Women, trained America's "second

The Seeds of Victory
Insure *the* Fruits of Peace

For Free Book Write to

NATIONAL WAR GARDEN COMMISSION
WASHINGTON, D.C.

Charles Lathrop Pack *Pres.*   Percival S. Ridsdale *Sec'y.*

Uncle Sam wanted *you* to plant a vegetable garden during World War I. (Illustrator Mabel Wright Enright was Frank Lloyd Wright's sister.)

The National War Garden Commission set up demonstration gardens throughout the country, including this one in New York City. Photograph by Frances Benjamin Johnston.

Henrietta Stout—dahlia breeder, author, founding member of the Short Hills Garden Club, New Jersey, and first president of the American Dahlia Society—sold her 'Sunshine' dahlia tubers to benefit the Red Cross.

line of defense" for the Women's Land Army. Its officers and "farmerettes" mobilized with rake and hoe to work on farms whose men had gone off to fight.

Women were organizing for more than gardening. The sheep peacefully grazing in the backyard of the White House offset the female furor out front. Every day starting in 1917, members of the National Woman's Party picketed along the fence that bounded the North Lawn. The Great War ended with the Armistice in 1918, but still the sentinels marched. They marched until the Nineteenth Amendment, guaranteeing all American women the right to vote, passed both House and Senate in June 1919.

In 1920, silver-haired Warren Harding won the first election in which his wife could vote for him. The Hardings used the White House grounds as

A young girl hands roses to suffrage pickets in front of the White House fence in 1917.

Laddie Boy, the Hardings' celebrity Airedale, photographed in 1922 just outside the Rose Garden.

This newspaper photograph was captioned "Waiting for Laddie Boy."

Between the wars, the White House grounds reopened for events such as the annual Easter Egg Roll, a favorite for children and a horror for the horticultural staff.

venues for parties and publicity. President Harding was, after all, an Ohio newspaperman, and both he and First Lady Florence Harding knew how to work the press. After the lean years of Wilson's wartime administration, Harding had promised a "return to normalcy" and that included the horticultural kind. His first official act was to reopen the gates to the White House grounds, closed since the war. The Hardings revived the ever-popular White House garden parties. They greeted disabled veterans under a tent among the roses. They accompanied Madame Marie Curie down the honeysuckle-edged steps to introduce her to the crowd. They appeared with their popular Airedale terrier, Laddie Boy, a dog that America fell for "to beat the band."

It was the Jazz Age. The first radio played in the White House halls. The Hardings reinstituted weekly Marine Band concerts, complete with jazz tunes, on the White House grounds. Hemlines rose. Florence Harding wore so many dresses in her favorite shade of blue, that in 1922 W. Atlee Burpee

Spring in the East Garden in the 1920s is full of peonies, pansies, and irises in this hand-colored glass slide by Frances Benjamin Johnston.

introduced a new variety of sweet pea in "Harding Blue." Yet there is no record of sweet peas planted at the Harding White House, and President Harding died suddenly of a heart attack the following year. His vice president, Calvin Coolidge, served out the remainder of Harding's term.

The twenties roared into the White House grounds in holiday attire when Calvin and Grace Coolidge turned on the first National Christmas Tree in the center of the Ellipse in 1923. The tree was illuminated by 2,500 red, green, and white lights supplied by the boosterish Electric League of Washington, an early example of holiday commercialism gone large. But the next year, the elegant Grace and "Silent Cal" suffered a deep loss that originated on the White House grounds. Their younger son, sixteen-year-old Cal Junior, got a blister while playing a tennis match. The blister turned into blood poisoning, and he died on July 7, 1924, at Walter Reed General

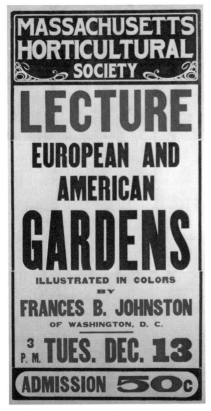

American gardens take an equal footing with European in Johnston's lecture to the Massachusetts Horticultural Society in 1927.

During a unique garden project in the 1920s, visitors were encouraged to pick the spring pansies before White House gardeners installed summer begonias.

Hospital. From then on, the gardener brought Grace Coolidge a red rose each morning to put in a vase beneath her son's portrait.

The plants in the White House garden kept growing through the years, as plants do. In 1928 Frederick Law Olmsted Jr., still employed by the successor to Senator McMillan's Commission, wrote an extensive letter to Colonel Ulysses S. Grant III, grandson of his namesake president and successor to Colonel Cosby, at the Office of Public Buildings and Grounds. Olmsted was direct. Anyone of taste, he wrote, "would have to rate the White House grounds as distinctly disappointing." He saw potential, particularly around

A White House gardener picks fruit from an ancient apple tree in the 1920s.

the South Lawn where the space could balance the grace of the building while serving the "amenities of family and social life." The history of the landscape should be studied and treated "with the utmost respect for what is good and fine in the old design." He underscored that "the White House grounds ought to be such that an organization like the Garden Club of America would proudly and unhesitatingly point them out to its members or to foreign visitors of kindred interests as among the best hundred examples of residential grounds in America."

Mrs. Hoover's new flagstone patio awaiting guests.

But Olmsted's ideas would have to wait. The Coolidges moved out of the White House, and the Hoovers moved in. First Lady Lou Hoover had a small bluestone terrace installed under the Jackson magnolia. With comfortable white furniture, it was a perfect place to breakfast in summer, to sit and knit or chat with her friends. It was a secluded outdoor room in a very public place, a small nod to the Arts and Crafts or "American Craftsman" movement. This early-twentieth-century style advocated for, among other things, the integration of indoor and outdoor spaces. The idea, wrote Gustav Stickley, was to "bring the garden and house into such intimate companionship that one hardly knows where one leaves off and the other begins."

For most of Hoover's single term, though, the stock market crash of 1929 and the resulting Great Depression took attention as well as appropriations away from garden endeavors at the White House and most American homes. It wasn't until the first of Franklin D. Roosevelt's four terms that Frederick

"*it's thrifty to grow your own*"

PETER HENDERSON & CO.
35 Cortlandt St.   *(Read Page 1)*   NEW YORK

During the Great Depression, seed catalogs emphasized the economic benefits of food gardening, such as this illustration in Peter Henderson's 1933 Annual.

Law Olmsted Jr. got his wish. In 1935, Olmsted and his firm delivered a landscape management plan for the White House.

Olmsted had researched the history of the landscape in detail and mapped its hundreds of trees and shrubs. The resulting design was not elaborate, appropriate given the nation's continuing economic hard times. It reorganized the South Lawn. An old Irish yew obstructing the view was removed. Out went the twenty flowering cherry trees that Helen Taft had planted around the South Fountain. In went additional plantings to enclose the private spaces on the grounds. Olmsted replaced the fiddle-shaped south

Neither snow nor rain nor heat nor gloom of night stays the White House gardeners in the completion of their appointed rounds.

Olmsted's design continued to emphasize the lawn, both north and south of the White House.

Horticulture jobs at the White House often require elaborate engineering, such as this project in the 1930s. Architect Charles McKim had suggested topiaried trees to adorn the upper terraces after the 1903 renovations, and they have been used ever since.

drive, reminiscent of Mount Vernon and in place since Andrew Jackson's time, with a simpler, more modern semicircle. At about the same time, the West Wing expanded upward to accommodate the growing New Deal staff and the Oval Office moved to its present location.

When their Britannic majesties, King George VI and Queen Elizabeth, the Queen Consort, came to stay in the White House in June 1939, Eleanor Roosevelt explained to the staff that the water should be chilled but served without ice, the English preference, for the events. It was the first visit of a reigning British monarch to the White House. Roosevelt worried how presidential gardens would rate in comparison to those of the British monarchy.

Looking outside her White House window, she wrote, "The railings of the steps leading down to the garden are covered with honeysuckle in bloom and the big magnolia tree planted by Andrew Jackson has opened wide its blossoms. England is a land of beautiful gardens and flowers, but I do not think the magnolia will be duplicated there." Her humor broke through when she mentioned, "Franklin, Jr. brought his Great Dane to stay until he takes him to Hyde Park, which will add a homelike touch to the South Lawn."

Peace did not last, at home or abroad. In September 1939, three months after the royal visit, Britain and France declared war on Germany in response to Hitler's invasion of Poland. America entered the war immediately after the attack on Pearl Harbor in December 1941.

On the home front, there was the return of the war garden, now called the more upbeat "victory garden." The secretary of agriculture announced,

Eleanor Roosevelt with a basket of snapdragons, kneeling in front of the tulip bed by the South Portico for Children's Health Day in 1934.

Diana Hopkins with her father and stepmother, Louise Macy Hopkins, taking care of her victory garden on the South Lawn in 1943.

"Food Production is War Production!" enlisting all Americans to dig and grow for Uncle Sam. "Your Victory Garden will cut down on the amount of food that must be shipped for you and will help to keep the guns and tanks and planes rolling toward the war fronts," promised the *Victory Garden Campaign.* Eleanor Roosevelt judged the Victory Garden Show at Horticultural Hall in Boston in September 1942, with entries ranging from suburban-sized vegetable plots to city gardeners with window boxes. Some of the White House roses were replaced the following spring with a victory garden, tended not by the first lady but by presidential advisor Harry Hopkins's daughter, Diana.

For the general public, the White House grounds were cordoned off. Blackout curtains were installed, though FDR resisted the suggestion to

In April 1943, Donald Duck and his nephews, Huey, Dewey, and Louie, set off to plant in "The Victory Garden," from *Walt Disney's Comics and Stories #31*.

repaint the exterior in camouflage. Head gardener William Reeves did his best to keep up the appearances of the presidential precincts. In August 1944, Eleanor Roosevelt wrote that Reeves "managed to keep the little garden near the house looking very lovely. I enjoyed looking out this morning on the rose garden. . . . The flower beds on the lawn down by the tennis courts are not quite so well kept as usual, since labor is hard to find. But on the whole I think the grounds are a joy to see." She looked forward to the day "when the gates will be open again, and people can wander around even under the porte-cochère and view closely the house which belongs to all American citizens."

That day wasn't far off, but the Roosevelts would not be at the White House to see it.

America
the Beautiful

❧

We have always cultivated roses
in our gardens.

RONALD REAGAN, in a proclamation naming
the national floral emblem, 1986

1940S–1990S

(1945–1953) HARRY AND ELIZABETH "BESS" TRUMAN

(1953–1961) DWIGHT AND MAMIE EISENHOWER

(1961–1963) JOHN AND JACQUELINE KENNEDY

(1963–1969) LYNDON AND CLAUDIA "LADY BIRD" JOHNSON

(1969–1974) RICHARD AND THELMA "PAT" NIXON

(1974–1977) GERALD AND ELIZABETH "BETTY" FORD

(1977–1981) JAMES AND ROSALYNN CARTER

(1981–1989) RONALD AND NANCY REAGAN

(1989–1993) GEORGE H. W. AND BARBARA BUSH

H ARRY S. TRUMAN stepped into the presidency reluctantly, and his wife, Bess, had a definite distaste for "First Ladying." Roosevelt had died during his fourth term in April 1945, a few weeks before victory was declared in Europe. Left at the helm for the atomic bomb, the Marshall Plan, the Berlin Airlift, and the start of the Cold War, it is small wonder that President Truman once told his wife that the executive residence felt like "the great white jail."

At least the gardeners were happy. Some presidents—Hoover was infamous in this regard—wanted the help to be invisible. Not so with President Truman. "Mr. Truman was the most insistent that we be at ease," wrote longtime White House maid Lillian Parks. But no one had told this to the garden staff who "were still crouching behind the rose bushes when they saw the President approach on the way to his office. Truman asked, 'Why are these people peeping at me?'" After that the gardeners kept working when the president passed by.

Indoors, the White House was about to fall down. The extensive remodeling done during Teddy Roosevelt's administration had some basic structural problems that started to surface, not the least of which was a dearth of proper foundations. Plaster fell. Walls cracked. Floors creaked. The presidential bathtub started sinking into the tile floor. Things went from ominous to obvious when the leg of daughter Margaret Truman's spinet piano broke

The dapper Truman admires a star magnolia on the South Lawn in 1946.

through an upstairs floor one summer day in 1948. Consulting engineers issued the red alert. The Trumans moved across Pennsylvania Avenue to Blair House, the official guest residence. Immediately. Over the next three and a half years, the White House was gutted, reinforced, and rebuilt. Construction chaos once again reigned in the White House gardens.

The Trumans had given much thought to a custom-built outdoor space at the White House. Earlier in 1948, before their peremptory relocation, Harry Truman had decided to have a porch. The porch on their home in Independence, Missouri, had been their favorite summer haunt, so why shouldn't the president of the United States enjoy the same? Jens Jensen, the midwestern landscape architect who worked with Frank Lloyd Wright and popularized the prairie style in parks and gardens, would have sided with Truman. "The spacious porch has the right to come into rank as a cardinal necessity of the country house," Jensen had written. "Any observer of country life cannot

Roots of one of the heirloom trees, carefully
excavated during construction.

fail to see that no part of the house is more used in summer than the cool,
clean, inviting porch."

At a cost of $15,000 and ignoring the criticism of architects and the Fine
Arts Commission alike, the president got his "outside breathing space." His
porch was actually a second-floor balcony, inserted behind the long columns
of the South Portico. Goodbye, awnings under which Theodore and Edith
Roosevelt had breakfasted. Hello, intimate space for presidential families,
protected from the public eye.

Blame it on Truman. Our American tendency to instant gardening grat-
ification made its first appearance at the White House in March 1952. The
Trumans were poised to move back in, just in time to receive the Queen of
the Netherlands. Standing near the North Portico one could see graders
"smoothing off a new front lawn just ahead of landscapers who were rolling

This 1952 view of the South Portico with the Truman balcony shows gardeners moving a southern magnolia from the west to the east side, opposite the Jackson magnolias. The *Kansas City Star* opined that it was nice to know that Truman would leave Washington with something balanced, if only the landscape.

A view from the Truman balcony, enhanced with potted geraniums.

down turf that had arrived in great truck loads." (The lawn had been excavated for central air conditioning, storage, and a bomb shelter.) In addition to rolling out the green carpet, White House gardeners installed a full-sized cherry tree. It was in bloom.

Up-to-date was what was wanted in American gardens, as returning veterans and their families created an explosion in suburban development. Out with the old and in with the new at the White House as well. As the moving vans carted back the furniture that had been in storage at the National Gallery, the grounds staff put in plants that were positively new-fangled. Azaleas included twenty-seven "of the most recent varieties propagated by the Agriculture Department at Beltsville [Maryland]." The Rose Garden was replanted "with the most modern varieties, including a general introduction of the popular Floribunda." The outside matched the inside of the White House. "Needless to say," Americans were told, "the Trumans are delighted with their new home, from the shiniest of modern electric kitchens to the tip of the new television aerial."

Sod awaits in rolls, and arrives with giant American boxwood from Gude Nursery in Rockville, Maryland, to replace the old Japanese holly hedge in front of the North Portico.

With all this worship at the altar of the modern, Truman was also alert to history. In the garden, a southern magnolia that President Wilson had planted was balled, burlapped, and transplanted. The antique bricks from the White House interior weren't reused in situ, but Truman sent 95,000 of them to Mount Vernon to restore George Washington's garden walls and orangery. Perhaps inspired by Mount Vernon, he had a new box hedge planted in front of the North Portico, loosely pruned to soften the façade's symmetry. It was like a typical foundation planting in front of an FHA-funded Cape Cod house in Levittown, only much bigger.

Since President Eisenhower's inaugural flight, Marine One has taken off and landed from the South Lawn.

Eisenhower, who became president in 1953, made two substantial disturbances—one athletic and the other aerodynamic—to Truman's new lawn. For practicing his beloved golf game, Ike had a putting green installed in 1954. And in 1957, the first helicopter took off from the South Lawn.

The putting green kept the gardeners busy, and not just with trimming the grass. The population of gray squirrels was wreaking havoc with the turf; thus a new policy of trap-and-transport was instituted. Staff captured squirrels with box traps and deported the captives to West Virginia. One senator started a "Save The White House Squirrels" fund. The president's response was "No comment."

It seems appropriate that Eisenhower, retired army general and the first Supreme Allied Commander in Europe, inaugurated Marine One as the latest executive transportation mode. One can almost hear the gardener sigh.

In 1954, Eisenhower worked with the United States Golf Association to install a putting green on the south side of the White House, though it is clear from this photograph that he practiced more than his putts.

The American love affair with the lawn fits well with golf though not, perhaps, with divots.

Washington Post cartoonist Herb Block depicted President Eisenhower and a White House squirrel battling over the putting green.

Robert Redmond, head gardener under Truman, Eisenhower, and Kennedy, looks happy in this 1949 article in *The Saturday Evening Post*, though it was before the advent of the helicopters at the White House.

"The White House head gardener is not a man to dictate to President Eisenhower," the *Milwaukee Journal* reported, "but he'd be happier if those helicopters would stop landing on his lawn. They burn the grass."

The American backyard was going upscale, and Ike's putting green was just one example. There were decks and driveways. The kidney-shaped swimming pool made its splashy debut in the California landscape with Thomas Church's design for the Donnell family. The Scotts company built a 123,000-square-foot plant to produce its new Turf Builder fertilizer in 1956. *Leave It to Beaver*, the prototype suburban television series, piloted on April 23, 1957. Its fictional family, the Cleavers, lived on shady Mapleton Street in the fictional suburb of Mayfield. The opening credits showed Mr. Cleaver trimming the hedges, Mrs. Cleaver carrying a tray with iced tea, and the two boys pushing lawn mowers. While not every American could boast a putting green or a helicopter, they could aspire to a perfect lawn, patio, barbecue grill, and an automobile to drive on one of the new interstates, commissioned by President Eisenhower through the Federal-Aid Highway Act.

Meanwhile, think Mamie, think pink. First Lady "Mrs. Ike" Eisenhower picked pink dresses. She redid her rooms at the White House in pink color schemes to the point that the help started calling it the "Pink Palace." With her signature bangs and preferred color, it wasn't long before a 'Mamie Pink' chyrsanthemum hit the nursery catalogs. Perhaps it evicted the 'Harding Blue' sweetpeas. But we must give Mamie her due as a thoughtful tradition-alist in the garden. She asked the gardener for red petunias around the South Fountain because the cannas grew eight feet tall and obscured the visitors' views. The cannas suddenly seemed a bit fuddy-duddy—too big, too garish, and just plain out of style.

Mamie Eisenhower's love of pink
extended to flowers.

From the standpoint of style, Camelot arrived at the White House in January 1961 in the form of the handsome President John Kennedy and the iconic First Lady Jacqueline Bouvier Kennedy. Jack and Jackie would prove to be America's quintessential power couple in terms of White House design, inside and out. While the first lady worked to transform "that dreary Maison

John and Jacqueline Kennedy stride across the South Lawn in 1962.

Blanche" into the "most perfect house in the United States," rescuing historic antiques from federal storage facilities and enlisting the aid of notables like decorator Dorothy "Sister" Parish and American furniture expert Henry Francis DuPont, the president gave some attention to the landscape.

First, there was the lawn. It was never quite right. "It is driving the President crazy," said Jacqueline Kennedy, "and I agree with him. In Glen Ora, [the Kennedy's weekend retreat in Middleburg, Virginia] where we have a man who cuts the lawn every two weeks, it looks like green velvet—and this place looks as well as cornfields in Virginia." National Park Service employees—by this time responsibility for the White House grounds had shifted from the Army Corps of Engineers—tried everything. There are even accounts of brown patches being spray-painted green before important guests arrived. Why hadn't Ike's gardener thought of that?

In 1961, the Kennedys' European state visit included stops in Austria and England. They were, as might be expected, royally received. President Kennedy was enamored of the glories of the June gardens: the Baroque beds of Schönbrunn in Vienna, where Kennedy met Nikita Khrushchev, and the English borders of the Windsors at Buckingham Palace. The gardens at the White House did not measure up. His feelings echoed Frederick Law Olmsted Jr.'s sentiments from three decades before. Kennedy turned to family friend Rachel Lambert Mellon, a serious gardener, to redo with dispatch the gardens that flanked the West Wing. "What gardener could resist?" wrote "Bunny" Mellon, and she, in turn, called in Washington landscape architect Perry Wheeler to assist. Once again, the West Garden, that rectangle formed by the South Portico and the low colonnades that flank the cabinet room and Oval Office, was to be redone.

If Oleg Cassini was Jacqueline Kennedy's "Secretary of Style" when it came to her clothes closet, Mellon held the same post for John Kennedy in the garden. Heir to the Lambert fortune—her grandfather Gerard Lambert invented Listerine, and her father founded Warner-Lambert—she was a self-taught and accomplished horticulturist and designer. The landscape she created for her Virginia home is justifiably famous. "This garden is made of love," she told *Vanity Fair* when describing Oak Spring, where she lived with her second husband, Paul Mellon, "and details. Look for the details."

The Rose Garden laid out with pegs and string before breaking ground.

Nineteenth-century horseshoes and shards from old greenhouse pots surfaced during soil preparation for the new garden.

The first plants in the ground were the largest—four saucer magnolias, transplanted from federal land near the Tidal Basin.

The newly planted beds with their trim layout.

She gave the same attention to detail to the White House Rose Garden. There were several design constraints. The center of the space was reserved for a lawn large enough to accommodate a thousand people at an event. The president wanted a small private terrace near the Oval Office for outdoor meetings. A new set of steps with a platform would allow him to be seen and heard above a crowd, introducing a sort of permanent theater into the garden space. For the plants themselves, Kennedy "loved flowers and asked if a variety of other types could be mixed with the roses." He had been reading Thomas Jefferson's garden notes and hoped for plants that would reflect Jefferson's tastes.

Mellon drew inspiration from a set of magnificent magnolias that anchor the Fifth Avenue façade of the Frick Museum on Manhattan's Upper East Side. Saucer magnolias with their silvery gray bark, open branching,

The 'Katherine' crabapples at peak.

and showy pink blooms were just the thing to make a statement at the White House. These she placed at the corners of her plan, then connected them with a "bone structure," as she called it, of long rectangular beds edged with a boxwood hedge of the hybrid 'Green Pillow'. She divided the rectangles with diagonals, outlining the resulting diamonds and triangles with the dark green of clipped English box and contrasting silver santolina. The American design pendulum had swung back to the traditional.

Two sets of 'Katherine' crabapples, a pinkish white double-flowering variety, lined the colonnades, like flowered buntings when they bloomed. The beds were anchored by roses, which Mellon noted as "the one flower that

President Kennedy proudly showing the Rose Garden to Princess Beatrix of the Netherlands in April 1963.

The Mercury astronauts receiving an award in a 1963 Rose Garden ceremony.

unites all the occupants through the history of the White House." Their running mates included tulips and grape hyacinths, pansies and lady's mantle, geraniums and lilies, heliotrope and chrysanthemums—a seasonal succession that would have pleased Thomas Jefferson. The garden, approximately 125 feet long and 60 feet wide, soaked up quantities of plants. Perry Wheeler's 1962 order to Blue Mount Nursery in Monkton, Maryland, requested more than 2,000 pansies: 1,000 dark blue, 650 light blue, 650 white, with just a dash of, you guessed it, 330 red.

The newly planted garden captured the country's collective imagination, just as Mrs. Kennedy's televised tour of the redecorated White House interior garnered a record fifty-six million viewers. The Rose Garden became the favorite setting for occasions such as the October 10, 1963, presentation to the seven astronauts of Project Mercury. Standing on the custom-made platform, President Kennedy and the honorees, including first-American-in-space Alan Shepard and future senator and presidential contender John Glenn, were framed by the crabapples and tidy rows of boxwood. The crowd of dignitaries and press corps fit comfortably in the space. Chrysanthemums added color to the event. It was a garden with the right stuff.

With the success of the Rose Garden, President Kennedy asked Mellon for an encore in 1962. The East Garden, long an outdoor room used by presidents' families, had not been reworked since the Wilson administration. A change was overdue. Mellon was willing, but in trying to come up with a design concept to drive the plan, she hit a wall. Then Jacqueline Kennedy mentioned wanting a small croquet court for her daughter, Caroline, then aged four, and toddler John Junior. Mellon's eureka moment came with the word "croquet." She took her inner child to work, remembering one of her favorite books, Lewis Carroll's *Alice in Wonderland*, in which Alice and the Queen of Hearts play croquet in a rose garden using live flamingoes for mallets. Some weeks before, Mellon had seen some unusual American holly topiaries at Gude Nursery in Rockville, Maryland. "They would make the outline for this new garden, and like Alice in Wonderland, the children could play surrounded by their high presence." There is something about a garden that sends us back to childhood—the wonders of discovery, the connection with the wide world.

Mellon discussed other ideas for the project with the first lady. They met near an elm tree planted by John Quincy Adams. Kennedy hoped that culinary herbs could be included to satisfy the needs of White House chef René Verdon. A grape arbor perhaps, decorated with hanging baskets of scented geraniums and pots of lemon verbena, could offer a shady, fragrant spot to read, entertain, and keep an eye on the children. A shallow pool with splashing water might add interest, auditory and otherwise.

Mellon incorporated these elements, planting herbs around the topiary, along with "children's flowers to pick as children do, taking the heads without the stems: marigolds, nasturtiums, pansies, and Queen Anne's lace." She had the arbor designed with hinged lattice windows opening to reveal the Washington Monument. The rectangular pool was augmented by American sculptor Sylvia Shaw Judson's bronze statue of a girl holding a watering can and trowel.

The topiaried hollies that provided Mellon's design hook for the East Garden have been growing there ever since.

Many of the shrubs and trees for the Rose Garden and the East Garden were sourced at Henry Hohman's Kingsville Nursery on Route 1 northeast of Baltimore. Hohman, a plantsman extraordinaire, specialized in unusual trees and shrubs. He was such a good propagator that a man who worked for him in the 1950s said that Hohman could get a broomstick to root. Hohman was known for his hybrids and cultivars, including the 'Green Pillow' boxwood used in the Rose Garden. He knew everybody who was anybody in plant circles around metro D.C., and Perry Wheeler was a close friend.

In the fall of 1963, Wheeler had been out to Kingsville to tag the boxwood for the East Garden project. The plants would stay in the ground until just before they were ready to be planted in the new garden. On November 23, 1963, Hohman wrote this poignant note to Wheeler, "Due to the occurrence of yesterday, our good President Kennedy being shot and killed, I will not make any move on the digging of the Boxwoods until I am advised by you that I should go ahead." He voiced the national reaction. "My feelings are inexpressible, and my entire system seems limp. This is an occurrence that will be in my mind for the rest of my days on earth." Work on the White House East Garden stopped.

The next year when Lady Bird Johnson told Jacqueline Kennedy that they intended to install the garden and name it for her, Kennedy protested that it had been her husband's project. She later relented. Mellon, with her "working-at-it" authority on all things horticultural, and Perry Wheeler with his technical finesse, worked with head gardener Irvin Williams and his staff to install the garden the following spring. Johnson officially dedicated the Jacqueline Kennedy Garden on April 22, 1965.

Beyond the White House grounds, Lady Bird Johnson is linked to beautification, though she never liked the word. "Always, always, I felt that I would give a special prize to whoever would give us a better word than 'beautification'! It sounds institutional, clinical, it doesn't have any of the joy of the work in it." Madison Avenue did a better job with sloganeering for the "Keep America Beautiful" campaign, which Johnson joined in 1965. The Highway Beautification Act, known as Lady Bird's Bill, gave the movement teeth,

The pergola, designed by Mellon's friend architect I. M. Pei, provided a shaded spot with a fine view of the Jacqueline Kennedy Garden.

Sylvia Shaw Judson's "Little Gardener" has always looked on to the Jacqueline Kennedy Garden. Judson is most famous for Savannah's "Bird Girl," the sculpture shown on the cover of the bestselling *Midnight in the Garden of Good and Evil*.

Lady Bird Johnson discusses city beautification projects for Washington D.C. in the State Dining Room. Secretary of the Interior Stewart Udall is on the left and conservationist Laurance Rockefeller is on the right.

A cartoonist in the 1970s took off on "Keep America Beautiful" in the spirit of Ogden Nash who wrote, "I think that I shall never see/A billboard lovely as a tree/Indeed unless the billboard falls/ I'll never see a tree at all."

banning billboards, junkyards, and other eyesores from the federal inter-
state system and encouraging wildflower planting. As a leader of the Committee for a More Beautiful Capital, she oversaw the planting of thousands of
bulbs around Washington and the replacement of aging cherry trees around
the Tidal Basin. Whatever one chooses to call it, Johnson's push for beautification brought a gentle environmentalism to the streets.

Johnson understood that beautification, that "tangled skein of wool,"
was part of a bigger picture: "recreation and pollution and mental health,

make
AMERICA
beautiful

with a Home Improvement Loan
from Tracy-Collins

Prospective loan applicants are urged to
beautify their homes with a promotional
packet of zinnia seeds.

and the crime rate, and rapid transit, . . . and the war on poverty, and parks—
national, state, and local." The 1960s saw the first great awakening of the
modern environmental movement, a decade of protest and change that
included Vietnam War protests and the March on Washington. Rachel Car-
son published *Silent Spring* in 1962. President Johnson signed the Endan-
gered Species Act and the Land and Water Conservation Act, among others.

The first lady also understood that the love of beauty, of gardening, often
germinates in childhood. Lady Bird Johnson's last addition to the grounds
was the Children's Garden, what she called their departing gift to the White
House. Unlike the Jacqueline Kennedy Garden, it was more private, tucked
in among the evergreen shrubs and trees. Edward Durell Stone Jr., a landscape architect and son of the architect who had designed the Kennedy

Vietnam War protestors outside the White House gates include Coretta Scott King and Dr. Benjamin Spock in 1967. Steel gates had replaced one pair of Hedl's wrought-iron originals in 1937, but the American Horticultural Society restored them for its headquarters in Alexandria, Virginia, in 2005.

Center for the Performing Arts, designed the garden. There was a goldfish pond—later fitted with some inconspicuous netting after one of the Johnson grandchildren fell in—miniature wrought-iron furniture, and a winesap apple tree that would be perfect for climbing. "I think of the spot as the sort of place a First Lady who is a grandmother might wheel a baby carriage and sit in the shade and enjoy her own back yard, in a quite secluded spot," Johnson wrote. "And very especially it would be a good place for four year olds to have a 'tea party,' or watch the goldfish in the little pool—or for their mother or grandmother to read about Peter Rabbit or Winnie-the-Pooh."

Home gardening, indoors and out, became part of pop culture. Television soon obliged, percolating new styles across the country at the speed of broadcast transmissions. Thalassa Cruso, aka "the Julia Child of Horticulture," hosted the quirky public television series *Making Things Grow* from 1966 to 1969 on WGBH-Boston. "People say I manhandle my plants," she said on one episode, whacking some overgrown houseplant out of its pot and bashing loose its rootball. "What could they possibly mean?" She was TV's first gardening personality, followed by James Underwood Crockett with *Crockett's Victory Garden* in the mid-1970s and Mel Bartholomew in *Square Foot Gardening* in the early 1980s.

Television coverage came into the White House gardens in a big way with the Nixons. On June 12, 1971, President Richard Nixon was the father of the bride, escorting his daughter Tricia Nixon up the aisle in the Rose Garden. Her wedding to Edward Cox was the Rose Garden's first. There were prime time special reports with taped highlights and guest commentators. On CBS, Dan Rather co-anchored with Lynda Bird Johnson Robb, who had been married at the White House, albeit indoors, four years before. The Rose Garden was pristine, with extra roses and gardenias brought in for the occasion. The weather cooperated, with the ceremony wedged between rain showers

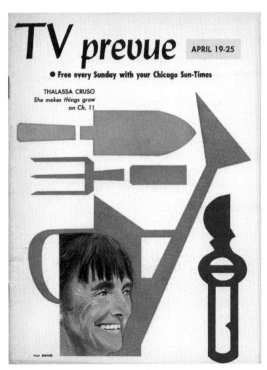

Thalassa Cruso, America's first television gardening personality.

President Nixon signals his approval to the orchestra after the marriage of his daughter Tricia to Edward Cox.

that dampened neither the bride's spirits nor her Priscilla of Boston dress.

The most vivid image of the Nixons on the White House grounds was, arguably, their last. The former president and first lady departed from the South Lawn in Marine One on August 9, 1974, after his resignation in the aftermath of the Watergate scandal, a scandal named for a building complex in turn named for a water gate on the old Chesapeake and Ohio Canal.

Nixon's resignation propelled Gerald R. Ford into the presidency. An avid swimmer, the president added an outdoor swimming pool to the White House grounds in 1975. He delighted the press corps by holding a news conference there, including a demonstration lap.

For the bicentennial, Ford hosted a Rose Garden dinner on July 7, 1976, during which he and Queen Elizabeth II toasted one another and their respective nations. The Queen's speech remembered the Revolutionary War, the first visit of John Adams to England as envoy to the Court of St. James,

President Ford acknowledges the toast of Queen Elizabeth at a dinner in the Rose Garden. Vice President Nelson Rockefeller raises his glass.

and then, bravely given her location that night, went on to the War of 1812 and its fiery results. "Mr. President," the Queen noted, "history is not a fairy tale. Despite the good intentions, hostility soon broke out between us—and even burst into this house. But these early quarrels are long buried. What is more important is that our shared language, traditions, and history have given us a common vision of what is right and just." What Her Majesty may not have known was that debris from the burnt White House buried in 1814 was unearthed during the excavation for President Ford's swimming pool.

If the White House gardens could talk and one knew how to listen, they might tell state secrets or children's stories. Jimmy Carter met with Egyptian president Anwar Sadat in the Rose Garden in 1980 not long after the signing of the Camp David Accords and subsequent Egyptian-Israeli peace treaty. On the lighter side, President Carter also had a simple platform tree house built for his tween daughter, Amy, among the branches of the blue atlas cedar on the South Lawn. She was known to use it for sleepovers with

President Carter and Egyptian President Anwar Sadat have a private discussion in what might be an early example of "Rose Garden strategy"; or "What is said in the Rose Garden stays in the Rose Garden."

friends, Secret Service oversight included. Caroline Kennedy's tree house had been more elaborate. It had a staircase with a handrail as well as a slide. But like many things related to the changing tenants of the White House, children's play equipment is removed at the end of the sitting president's term to make way for needs of a new first family.

Jimmy Carter propagated plants as well as peace and playhouses. He was a farmer, one of a handful of presidents since James Monroe who could legitimately list agriculture as his occupation in addition to politics. "Since we had planted pine, maple, and other trees around the White House from our Georgia farm," Carter remembered, "I asked for cuttings and seedlings

Jimmy Carter reaches for his grandson Jason from
his daughter, Amy, in the branches of the great
cedar on the South Lawn.

to carry home with us to Plains. We planted Andrew Jackson magnolias,
Harry Truman boxwoods, and also lindens, hemlock, goldenrain trees, and
an American elm in our yard."

Of the various cuttings that Carter chose, perhaps it is surprising that
he did not mention taking White House roses to represent his years in the
executive mansion. Ronald Reagan, the Great Communicator, would make
official the significance of the rose. In 1986, President Reagan declared the
rose as the national floral emblem of the United States of America. The proclamation included these words: "For the love of man and woman, for the love
of mankind and God, for the love of country, Americans who would speak
the language of the heart do so with a rose. . . . The White House itself boasts
a beautiful Rose Garden. We grow roses in all our fifty States. We find roses

Twenty-plus years before Ronald Reagan was elected president, he anchored the Tournament of Roses Parade in South Pasadena, California. It seems fitting that rose-grower Jackson & Perkins named two new cultivars 'Nancy Reagan' and 'Ronald Reagan' in their honor.

throughout our art, music, and literature. We decorate our celebrations and parades with roses. Most of all, we present roses to those we love, and we lavish them on our altars, our civil shrines, and the final resting places of our honored dead."

One wishes the Bushes, President George H. W. and First Lady Barbara, had made bigger changes to the gardens at the White House, particularly given their surname. They would have joined the ranks of other appropriately named American gardeners such as Allen Bush (no relation), the plantsman whose wife, Rose, enjoys introducing herself at garden conferences, and Todd Forrest, Vice President of Horticulture at the New York Botanical Garden. And it might have been. Barbara Bush is an avid gardener at her home in Kennebunkport, Maine. She was also a member of the Garden

The open Ellipse and clear view across the South Lawn as envisioned by Frederick Law Olmsted, Jr. appears in this display of the AIDS Memorial Quilt in 1988.

Club of America, as was her mother, who served as chair of its Conservation Committee, and her daughter-in-law, Laura, who would later become first lady. But Barbara Bush left the gardening to the "very talented National Park Service staff," and did "the next best thing: take long walks around the grounds every single day and enjoy the flowers."

Rather than change, garden preservation was in the air. The Garden Conservancy, founded in 1989—the same year Bush took office—was formed to "preserve exceptional American gardens for the education and enjoyment of the public." And what are the White House gardens, if not exceptional? *Martha Stewart Living*, which previewed in 1991, and her *Gardening Month by Month*, published the same year, promoted traditional motifs—the herb garden, the rose garden, the flower garden—already well-represented at the White House. The presidential gardens were impeccably well-kept, emphasizing tradition rather than innovation.

Still, there were some additions to the grounds during George H. W. Bush's administration. A newly installed horseshoe pit became a favorite of staff as well as senators. A small ornamental pool was put in near the West Wing terrace and stocked with goldfish that were forever being eaten by raccoons. Unfortunately the raccoons' fishing expeditions also tended to trip the alarm systems.

No garden is immune to pests. White House head gardener Irvin Williams described some of the elaborate non-lethal tactics used to deter the evil empire of garden herbivores. Fertilizer laced with Louisiana hot sauce discouraged moles and voles. Bushel baskets of Georgia peanuts were strapped to tree trunks to distract marauding squirrels from the precisely planted tulip bulbs. "We go through hundreds of pounds of peanuts each season," reported Williams. One garden writer called this a "policy of appeasement," though an organic gardener might have dubbed it a lure crop.

There has been a perpetual love-hate relationship with squirrels on the White House grounds. In the 1920s, one squirrel was so tame that members of the press corps nicknamed him "Pete." Sixty years later President Reagan brought acorns from Camp David on a regular basis to feed the squirrels in the Rose Garden. In 1989, after packing up the Oval Office to make way for George Bush, Reagan had left a note on the desk that opened with, "Don't let the turkeys get you down" and another outside the door for

Two presidents, George H. W. Bush and Nursultan Nazarbayev of Kazakhstan, take a break to pitch horseshoes at the White House in 1992.

"Pete" the tame squirrel, accepting a handout in 1922.

the squirrels reading "Beware of the dog," referring to Millie, the Bushes' English springer spaniel.

As in any garden some wildlife was welcome, like the pair of mallards that returned to swim in the South Fountain every spring with the regularity of State of the Union speeches. And, as in any garden, nothing lives forever. An ancient elm, believed to be one of the seedlings nurtured by John Quincy Adams in the 1820s, was terminally weakened after a second lightning strike and reluctantly removed in 1991. First Lady Barbara Bush planted a replacement, a sapling propagated by White House gardener Irv Williams. He grafted a tender cutting from the Adams original tree onto new rootstock. It just might be a metaphor for America.

The American elm propagated from the John Quincy Adams original.

Is Green the New
Red, White, and Blue?

∽

The City of Magnificent Intentions.

CHARLES DICKENS, 1842

1990S AND BEYOND

(1993–2001) WILLIAM AND HILLARY CLINTON
(2001–2009) GEORGE W. AND LAURA BUSH
(2009–2016) BARACK AND MICHELLE OBAMA

A GARDEN CAN BE a canvas for commemoration. In the case of First Lady Hillary Clinton, thoughts of sculpture and gardens conjured memories of her first date with her future husband. They met in the registration line at law school. They walked and talked and ended up at the Yale Art Gallery, admiring a Henry Moore exhibition in the outdoor sculpture yard. Years later in 1993, when she and President Bill Clinton became the new occupants of the White House, the Jacqueline Kennedy Garden resonated for her. "When I moved in here, and started wandering around the various parts of the house and yards and gardens, I kept coming back to that garden," Clinton said, "which I found restful and private. I spent a lot of time there, sitting in the little trellised area, or out on one of the stone benches, and it just looked to me like a garden that should have some sculpture in it. It looked as though at some point someone had landscaped it with that in mind."

The topiary hollies and formal plantings designed by Bunny Mellon and Perry Wheeler were themselves sculptural. The trees and shrubs formed niches that seemed purpose-built. Now the mature garden became a stage for eight exhibitions of the works of living American sculptors, drawn from regional museums. Seven were funded by a private foundation; the eighth, showcasing Native American artists, was underwritten by the Heard Museum in Phoenix. The White House setting created some unusual

Bill and Hillary Clinton surrounded by "Voltri XV" by artist David Smith in the Jacqueline Kennedy Garden in 1996.

hurdles. Each sculpture had to be cleared by the Secret Service, and the winds kicked up by helicopters had to be considered. One can imagine the White House gardeners holding their collective breaths as the crane moved each piece into place.

A garden injects nature into the experience of sculpture—leaves and petals, trunks and branches, sun and shade. American gardens have long served as sculpture venues. Permanent installations range from Brookgreen Gardens in South Carolina, founded by Archer and Anna Hyatt Huntington in 1932 to showcase her work, to the Sculpture Gardens at the PepsiCo Corporate Headquarters, created in the 1970s by then CEO Donald M. Kendall in Purchase, New York. There are temporary installations like Christo and Jeanne Claude's 2005 project "The Gates" in Central Park and Dale Chihuly's sculptural glassworks in an array of public gardens, most recently at

Andrew Jackson atop his horse, Duke, has looked to the White House from Lafayette Square since its 1853 dedication by Stephan A. Douglas. Since then, newer castings have been placed in Jackson Square in New Orleans; in Nashville at the Tennessee State Capitol Building; and in downtown Jacksonville, Florida.

botanic gardens in Phoenix and Denver. (Chihuly, in 1999, also made two "Crystal Trees of Light" from blown glass to help usher in the new millennium at the White House.) There are memorials. In Washington D.C. you will find many. The 1852 Andrew Jackson equestrian statue by Clark Mills perpetually doffs his hat atop a rearing horse diagonally across from the White House in Lafayette Square. The 1982 Vietnam Veterans Memorial Wall designed by Maya Lin cuts a black vein into the grass of the Mall. Of the sculpture installations at the White House, Hillary Clinton wrote, "I often find myself going out of my way to walk through the gardens during the day. Each time, I feel energized by the spirit of those who spend their lives adding beauty to our surroundings and freeing our imaginations."

Under President George W. Bush and First Lady Laura Bush, the Jacqueline Kennedy Garden returned to its classic look. Artists were commissioned, but for smaller interior projects. In 2001 the White House engaged fifty artists to create holiday ornaments—miniatures of period buildings from each state—to decorate a historic preservation-themed Christmas tree for the Blue Room. But that December in the aftermath of the September 11 terrorist attacks, the usual public tours were cancelled. "That season," said Laura Bush, "the White House had the quality of stillness after a snow."

In a post–September 11th world, access to the grounds changed. Security concerns closed Pennsylvania Avenue in front of the White House to vehicular traffic. This presented an unusual design opportunity, an opportunity given to one of a new generation of American landscape architects, Michael Van Valkenburgh, the Charles Eliot Professor of Landscape Architecture at Harvard's Graduate School of Design.

Van Valkenburgh and his firm, MVVA, took the Pennsylvania Avenue project in 2002; it was opened in November 2004. He had to balance "the L'Enfant Plan, . . . the naturalism of Andrew Jackson Downing's Lafayette Park and the informality of the White House grounds." Just as he had done at Princeton University, Brooklyn Bridge Park in New York, and Maggie Daley Park in Chicago, he and his firm managed to look both ways, back in history and forward to future needs, for this particular street. While there are security bollards, they are discreetly placed in a sleek, modern paving pattern. It is a promenade for people, including protestors exercising their First Amendment rights. Historic fixtures light the way for evening strollers.

An aerial shot of Pennsylvania Avenue in 2007 with Michael Van Valkenburgh's design.

Traditional benches line the pedestrian paths for those who wish to contemplate, or merely to rest. New disease-resistant American elms make their own parade, marching in double and single file ranks along Pennsylvania Avenue.

Inside the fence, a disease-resistant American chestnut joined the elms in an attempt at a comeback. President Bush planted a specimen on the North Lawn to mark the 133rd National Arbor Day. Once keystone species of the eastern North American forests, the chestnut and elm were nearly wiped out by fungal blights introduced in the early part of the twentieth century. Scientists and gardeners continue to work on effective controls and new hybrids, while addressing new challenges such as the pine beetle, emerald ash borer, and Asian longhorn beetle.

Gardens grow. And grow. By 2004, the forty-year-old Rose Garden was showing its age. The 'Katherine' crabapples were shading out the roses, so

Laura Bush, holding a rose named in her honor, smiles at Bill Williams from Jackson & Perkins, the rose hybridizer.

Seasonal plantings change in the Rose Garden each year. Magenta gomphrena and orange celosia are ready to go in to provide fall color.

that fresh rose bushes had to be brought in like annuals each year to ensure a good bloom. Laura Bush, like her mother-in-law, had come from a long line of gardeners, and she encouraged an update. Dale Haney, the incumbent head gardener, and his team replaced the crabapples, the old boxwood, and the linden trees along the colonnade with new, young specimens of the original selections. The gardeners also obliged by planting buckets of Texas bluebonnets, one of the first lady's favorites, for a spring display in the Rose Garden. Described by National Public Radio as a "closet preservationist," Bush laughed and said, "Well, not a closet preservationist. I'm a very active preservationist. . . . On our ranch, we're right now cultivating 50 acres of little blue stem which was the original prairie grass that would have been there."

Original prairie. Original plants. In the last quarter of the twentieth century, a national conversation arose about native plants and original habitats. Many landscape architects, starting with the Washington D.C. firm Oehme, van Sweden & Associates, created bold statements of grasses and perennials styled as "The New American Garden." Universities established schools of ecology. Habitat restorations got underway, reaching from Alaska's tundras and Hawaii's rainforests to Minnesota's prairies and Alabama's wetlands.

Michelle Obama took a shovel to the South Lawn in 2009 to make a food garden. Edible gardening was the fastest growing market segment according to the National Gardening Survey. The location of the new garden, tucked to the side of the South Lawn, adhered to the 1935 Olmsted plan, keeping the vista across the South Fountain clear. The plant selections reached back through history to some of the previous occupants of the house and grounds.

Assistant White House Chef Sam Kass visited Monticello during the garden's planning phase. He came back with seeds and plants of varieties that Jefferson grew in his own garden in Charlottesville: lettuce varieties like 'Tennis-ball' and 'Brown Dutch', prickly seeded spinach, 'Choux de Milan' cabbage, 'Green Globe' artichokes, and 'Marseilles' figs. With more than fifty varieties of vegetables, the new White House garden brought local food to the president's kitchen, in the same way the gardens had helped to feed earlier administrations like those of James Madison and Abraham Lincoln.

The White House Kitchen Garden was planted as a sort of national demonstration garden to promote healthy eating, especially for children,

Dale Haney, White House superintendent of grounds, looks on with a group of school children while Michelle Obama breaks ground for the Kitchen Garden in 2009.

Heirloom cabbage and lettuce look ready for harvest by April. The plant labels are the work of the White House calligraphers.

Michelle Obama and an attentive helper plant herbs for the Kitchen Garden's first growing season.

taking up a banner long held aloft by chefs like Alice Waters and writers like Michael Pollan. It is part of First Lady Michelle Obama's "Let's Move" initiative. A few lucky school groups get to dig in the garden, planting and harvesting, then helping to cook and eat veggie pizza. Sesame Street's Elmo and Rosita joined in one October. In the spring of 2011, American Indian children planted the traditional "three sisters" combination of corn, beans, and squash that John Smith saw on his Potomac expedition.

Some of the vegetables are selected with children in mind. Colorful heirloom tomatoes beckon. Long, skinny purple pole beans are invitations to small fingers. Harvesting peanuts is a guaranteed way to learn that they don't grow on trees and the basis for a lesson about George Washington Carver, American scientist and inventor, and promoter of the peanut.

The new garden set more than the media abuzz. White House carpenter Charlie Brandt, who kept hives at home, added beekeeper to his job

Tomatoes originated in South and Central America, were carried to Europe with sixteenth-century explorers, then made the return trip to North America. Thomas Jefferson grew them at Monticello, the Clintons grew them in a rooftop container garden at the White House, and since 2009 they have grown in the Kitchen Garden on the South Lawn. Drawing by Wendy Hollender.

description. The hives are the first on record at the White House. Like the sculpture installations, the hives are secured—strapped down—to withstand air turbulence from Marine One. The colonies prospered and produced 140 pounds of honey in their first year, used in the White House kitchen and for state gifts. Along with excess produce from the garden, some of the honey was also donated to Miriam's Kitchen, a nonprofit serving D.C.'s homeless.

Not everything was easy. "New garden" is synonymous with "learning experience." Because the beds weren't raised, Washington's summer thunderstorms washed them out. The next season, gardeners installed an edging of wooden boards to hold the soil. Every year, the garden changed and improved. By 2011 Peter Hatch, the Monticello über-gardener who had participated in the spring planting, wrote, "The soil was remarkable—it smelled

The garden's raised beds bearing their bounty.

good, the earthworms were everywhere, and it was humus rich and friable. If you judge a civilization by its soil, then, by the standards of the White House kitchen garden, we're making real progress." Hatch also planted beet seeds at the White House that March day in a gesture he termed slightly subversive. President Obama doesn't like beets, just as President George H. W. Bush didn't like broccoli.

If a civilization is judged by its garden traditions, the Tidal Basin's cherry trees have a story to tell. The year 2012 marked the centennial of Helen Taft's project. The planting had survived the "Cherry Tree Rebellion" in 1938, when protestors chained themselves to trees slated to be removed for the Jefferson Memorial. (A promise of new trees to frame the memorial broke the stalemate.) It had survived America's entrance into World War II when four trees were axed in 1941 in the days following Pearl Harbor. (For public relations

A pollinator bed, filled with bug- and bird-friendly plants native to the mid-Atlantic, is a recent addition to the Kitchen Garden. Joe Pye weed, turtlehead, blackeyed Susan, sneezeweed, cardinal flower, and butterfly weed spill out in late summer as Jim Adams, supervisory horticulturist, walks by.

The White House honeybees work the blooms of *Salvia* 'Black and Blue' in the Jacqueline Kennedy Garden.

purposes, the trees were temporarily referred to as "Oriental" until the end of the war.) The planting had survived a trio of beavers who, in the spring of 1999, decided that the Tidal Basin was the perfect place to settle and that cherry trees were the perfect building materials for a new dam. (The beavers were trapped and relocated, courtesy of the National Park Service.)

Through the years, cherry trees had died and new trees had been planted, including four hundred propagated from cuttings of the original 1912 donation. On March 27, 2012, one hundred years to the day from Helen Taft's planting, First Lady Michelle Obama planted a centennial cherry tree. She was accompanied by, among others, the Japanese ambassador, the secretary of the interior, and William H. Taft IV, the Tafts' great-grandson. Thinking forward, she told onlookers, "the First Lady—or the First Gentleman—of 2112 will also have the privilege of joining with our friends from

The view from the Rose Garden across the flowering grounds and South Lawn would make any gardener proud.

Japan, and planting another tree which will bloom for yet another one hundred years and beyond."

Like trees, seeds can be goodwill ambassadors. Seeds are beginnings, encapsulated hope. In 2014, President Obama made a state visit to Rome's new pontiff carrying a box of seeds, his gift to Pope Francis. They were not just any seeds, but paper packets of heirloom varieties grown in the White House garden. They were presented in a handcrafted chest made from wood reclaimed from the Baltimore Basilica, the first cathedral built in the United States. "If you have a chance to come to the White House, we can show you our garden as well," Obama offered. Francis responded with a Spanish phrase that could be translated as "Why not?" or "For sure." In September 2015, the president welcomed the pope to the White House in a ceremony on the South Lawn.

Why shouldn't the White House gardens be our common ground, a way to look forward into the future and back through the layers of American landscape design and garden history? The gardens are one of the oldest continually cultivated patches on the North American continent. In March of 1842, as part of his first American tour, Charles Dickens visited the White House and its gardens about which he was complimentary (for Dickens), though he said they had "the uncomfortable air of having been made yesterday." It was a new garden in a new city, a youth that had not reached maturity. That is no longer true. Of the city of Washington he wrote, "It is sometimes called the City of Magnificent Distances, but it might with greater propriety be termed the City of Magnificent Intentions."

Perhaps magnificent intentions are the best way to describe the White House gardens, then and now. Perhaps magnificent intentions can describe American gardening at large. Across the fifty states, gardeners create, preserve, and restore. Gardens beautify, nourish, and memorialize. Long may they wave.

Visitors enjoy the White House grounds.

Epilogue

O**N A LOVELY** April morning my husband and I stood in line, clutching our tickets in front of the Treasury Department with a throng of other eager visitors. It was Garden Tour day at the White House, a semi-annual event. The timed queues, managed by National Park Service rangers and volunteers, rivaled Disney's. An intense sun anticipated summer, and we staked out a spot of shade near the Civil War memorial to the south and east of the White House. Children played on the memorial's steps, lightly supervised by their caregivers. The variety of faces around us was an unscientific sample of the American citizenry. As our turn was called, an orderly process of security checks released us onto the White House grounds.

I had been gathering up this garden for months, sitting at my keyboard or in front of books and boxes in libraries and archives. While it wouldn't be my last visit to the grounds, it was the first. Until now I had only glimpsed the actual garden through the bars of the tall iron fence, like some pensive zoo visitor on days when the bears refuse to come out of their dens. The grounds danced in my head through period pictures and memoirs, letters and newspaper articles, ancient account books and YouTube videos.

And here it was. As we walked up the rise, it seemed obvious why George Washington sited the house where he did. To the left rose the so-called Jefferson mounds, though historians no longer agree that our third president designed them. Still, Thomas Jefferson would have endorsed their arcadian intent, the way the rounded berms hide and reveal, adding surprise to the experience of the grounds.

It is not the garden of a palace. The only crowns in evidence are the crowns of trees. On either side of the drive rose generations of trees, trees

Commemorative trees are celebrated on the White House grounds with labels added during Jimmy Carter's administration.

planted by a parade of presidents and first ladies. A huge ginkgo was just leafing out. A single redbud bloomed pink and white, a testament to some past gardener with a grafting knife. The Andrew Jackson magnolia, staked and cabled, looked none the worse for wear in spite of its being wounded by a small plane whose suicidal pilot aimed for the White House in 1994.

We were steeped in history. Mrs. Hoover's flagstone patio and Truman's porch both looked like pleasant places to be. Wisteria, climbing the iron railings of the South Portico, drooped with heavy lavender panicles. A cast-iron bench ordered by Millard Fillmore looked onto Eisenhower's putting green, though in fact George H. W. Bush had the green moved, then Bill Clinton had it redesigned and replaced in 1994. The view to the Washington Monument that Eleanor Roosevelt described and Frederick Law Olmsted Jr. specified

Wisteria makes its own cascade on the
South Portico railings.

was crisp and clear. The Monument itself was about to reopen after long and
complex repairs from a 5.8 magnitude earthquake in 2011.

If you have ever hosted or attended a garden tour, you will understand
the phrase, "You should have seen it last week." In the East, or Jacqueline
Kennedy Garden, the tulips and crabapples had just passed, their blossoms
yielding to a hot spell earlier that week. The topiary stood their ground,
and the lindens looked like a new planting, no doubt replacing the originals. There were hanging baskets of mixed edibles—pansies and lettuce,

variegated sage and trailing rosemary—that gave a nod to the interests of the current first lady. The Rose Garden, trim and elegant, with podium at the ready, seemed dwarfed given the scale of the building; it was hard to picture a thousand people seated comfortably at dinner within its perimeter.

The Obama daughters' play equipment was just outside the Oval Office, a homey touch, though I wondered if the girls had outgrown its slide and swings. I was glad to see, peering out from the shrubbery and in view of the president's windows, a life-sized statue of a male deer, complete with antlers. I had read an interview with Irv Williams, head gardener from the Kennedy to the George W. Bush administration, in which he gleefully reported placing the statue near the Oval Office as a salute to Harry Truman's slogan, "the buck stops here."

Some areas weren't accessible, as seems fitting for a house that is simultaneously public and private. The Lady Bird Johnson Children's Garden remained hidden. The swimming pool and basketball court were nowhere to be seen.

The Marine Band played, and visitors happily strolled, taking pictures, posing for friends, taking selfies. Perhaps they tweeted them to #whgarden, as a sign at the entrance had encouraged us to do. The Kitchen Garden was a great draw, with its burgeoning produce and beautiful signs, a vision of a productive potager. The beehives were busy, with pollinators and citizenry in peaceful coexistence. In the basin of the South Fountain, a pair of mallards paddled. As we left the grounds out of the gate to the southwest, we passed the gardeners' workshop with its small flotilla of John Deere equipment, lined up for the next shift. A mockingbird trilled overhead, perched in an elm tree.

First Gardeners

The Men Who Planted for Presidents

THESE HORTICULTURISTS WERE not name-droppers. Unlike many ushers, maids, and dressmakers through the decades, they did not publish memoirs, so in many cases the biographical record is sketchy. Perhaps this league of extraordinary gardeners simply preferred the trowel to the pen.

Thomas Magraw (?–?)

Served about eight years, to 1814, under James Madison.
Because of his part in saving the Gilbert Stuart "Lansdowne" portrait of George Washington from the White House in the hours before the British set the building on fire in 1814, the name of Thomas Magraw (sometimes spelled McGraw) has been passed down. He also appears earlier in Madison's 1811 accounting records, having picked up some casks of wine from an Alexandria merchant. Nothing else is known about him, at least not yet.

Charles Bizet (1778?–1850?)

Served 1817–1825, under James Monroe.
Charles Bizet was a gardener who knew three presidents. Born in France, Bizet was working in Virginia by 1810. James Monroe helped arrange a job for him with James and Dolley Madison. For the Madisons at Montpelier, Bizet designed a terraced, horseshoe-shaped garden near the house. To

install the garden, he directed the estate's slave workforce. Monsieur Bizet and his wife lived on the property. Mary Cutts, Dolley Madison's niece, remembered him as an experienced gardener who was a favorite with "his black aids," teaching some of them French. In 1817, Thomas Jefferson noted in a letter to Madison that "Besey" had stopped at Monticello for seeds. From 1817 until 1825, Bizet worked on the White House grounds, no doubt also directing a workforce made up at least in part of slaves. Bizet went back to Montpelier at the end of Monroe's term. Mary Cutts remembered him leaving Montpelier and returning to France shortly before Madison's death in 1836.

John Ousley (1795–1857)

Served 1825–1852, under John Quincy Adams, Andrew Jackson, Martin Van Buren, William Henry Harrison, John Tyler, James Polk, Zachary Taylor, Millard Fillmore, and Franklin Pierce.

An Irish immigrant who arrived in 1818 at Perth Amboy, New Jersey, John Ousley started at the executive mansion in 1825. His salary was $450 a year. John Quincy Adams mentioned Ousley a number of times in his diary during his presidential term. A lifelong scholar, our sixth president called Ousley his "nomenclator" because from him Adams learned the botanical names of plants. After John Quincy Adams's presidency, Ousley became a fixture at the White House. In the 1830s he won several prizes at the exhibitions of the Columbian Horticultural Society, including a silver cup made by W. A. Williams, a silversmith from Alexandria, Virginia. The public gardener for the District, James Maher, also worked on projects at the White House during this period, and for a short time one of Maher's friends, William Whelan, managed the White House vegetable garden. Ousley, presumably at retirement age, was dismissed during the Pierce administration.

John Watt (1824–1892)

Served 1852–1862, under Franklin Pierce, James Buchanan, and Abraham Lincoln.

John Watt, hailing from Scotland, became a naturalized citizen on April 18, 1853, during his White House service. Watt and his wife, Jane Masterson Watt, were both employed at the White House, he as head gardener, she as its first female usher. In 1857 he was the chairman of the Washington

Horticultural Society. He bought palms from greenhouses in New Jersey and ordered a giant water lily for the White House conservatory from Philadelphia in 1858. After his political intrigue and subsequent downfall during the Lincoln administration, and his brief stint as a seed inspector with the Patent Office, he appears to have left the horticultural field. After the Civil War, federal census and District of Columbia tax records show his occupation as "retail dealer" and "keeps boarding house."

George R. McLeod (1816?–1896)

Served 1862–1865, under Abraham Lincoln.
The second of three in a series of Scottish head gardeners at the White House, George McLeod stayed a short time. He resigned to open a nursery on twenty acres located on "the road leading from Shaw's Meeting House to the Baltimore-Washington Turnpike," what is now Montgomery Road in Beltsville, Maryland.

Alexander McKerichar (1831–1914)

Served 1865–1875, under Abraham Lincoln, Andrew Johnson, and Ulysses Grant.
Born in Perthshire, Scotland, Andrew McKerichar learned his trade as an apprentice in the gardens of the Duke of Atholl, near Dunkeld. In 1856 McKerichar was hired as outside foreman under John Watt, taking on the role of head gardener nine years later. Known for his hothouse grapes, he also raised off-season Caledonian cucumbers for President Grant. Like McLeod, he resigned from the White House to open a nursery business, his in Alexandria, Virginia. Perhaps running his own business did not suit him. In 1881 he was appointed superintendent of the Glenwood Cemetery. Glenwood, a landscaped cemetery in the style of Mount Auburn, is where "Mac" McKerichar lived and worked until his death more than forty years later and is his final resting place.

President Andrew Johnson once offered Alexander McKerichar a drink in honor of the hothouse grapes that the gardener had produced, and "Mac" accepted.

George Field (1846–1925)

Served 1875–1877, under Ulysses Grant.

The first English gardener at the White House, George Field's floral fame came after he left government employ and opened a nursery on Georgia Avenue NW with his brother Thomas. Field was responsible for naming and promoting the 'American Beauty' rose, originally selected on historian George Bancroft's estate as 'La Madame Ferdinande Jamin'. What's in a name, indeed. Field supplied the cattleya orchids for Alice Roosevelt Longworth's bridal bouquet in 1906. At the time *The Washington Post* described him as an orchid specialist. He was an active member of the Florist Club of Washington. In 1916, he sold his stock of orchid plants to W. J. and M. S. Vesey of Fort Wayne, Indiana, for $15,000.

Henry Pfister (1846–1925)

Served 1877–1902, under Rutherford B. Hayes, James Garfield, Chester Arthur, Grover Cleveland (1), Benjamin Harrison, Grover Cleveland (2), William McKinley, and Theodore Roosevelt.

A native of Zurich, Switzerland, Henry Pfister trained in the conservatories of a Swiss banker and at the Luxembourg Gardens in Paris as a young man. By the time he arrived in America in 1872, he was an experienced gardener in his late twenties. He made his way to Cincinnati, and then to Washington where he was hired under Hayes. Some sources say that he knew Rutherford and Lucy Hayes in Ohio. For the next quarter century he managed the burgeoning greenhouses, designed and planted the ornamental beds that punctuated the White House lawn, and provided all indoor floral and plant decorations, including for the wedding of Grover Cleveland and Frances Folsom. He was a regular contributor to garden periodicals and consulted with many leading lights of the horticultural world including Frederick Coville and Dr. Henry Nehrling. He was active with the Society of American Florists and was a horticultural judge at the World's Columbian Exposition of 1893. After the White House conservatories were removed during the Theodore Roosevelt renovation, Pfister was dismissed. He opened his own florist and landscape design business on Connecticut Avenue.

George Hay Brown (1838–1909)

Served 1902–1909, under Theodore Roosevelt.

The son of a landscape gardener, George H. Brown was born in Perthshire, Scotland, where he learned the family trade. In 1850, the family immigrated to the United States, settling first in Philadelphia. In 1858, Brown took a job in Washington D.C. at the government experimental gardens. During the Civil War he served with the Army Corps of Engineers in New Orleans and in the postbellum years lived in Missouri and Illinois. By 1890 he was back in Washington D.C. as a public gardener with the War Department. Brown rose through the ranks supervising work on the Capitol grounds, city parks, and the government propagating gardens and greenhouses near the Washington Monument, as well as the White House. He taught Theodore Roosevelt's children how to propagate plants in his greenhouses, and he was a proponent of public playgrounds for children. He died with his boots on. His obituary noted that he was a great aficionado of the poet Robert Burns. Brown is buried in Congressional Cemetery.

Charles Henlock (1856–1934)

Served 1909–1931, under William Taft, Woodrow Wilson, Warren Harding, Calvin Coolidge, and Herbert Hoover.

A Yorkshireman, Charles Henlock was proud of his horticultural training, having worked for Lord Mowbray in Yorkshire, Lord Denbigh in Warwickshire, and Lord Harrington in Derbyshire before spending five years in the employ of the Royal Horticultural Society. Henlock arrived in Washington D.C. just before President Cleveland's wedding in 1886 and was hired as a foreman gardener at the White House. Like George H. Brown before him, Henlock's responsibilities grew to encompass to the propagating gardens and city parks and reservations. Promoted to White House head gardener in 1909, Henlock supervised burning the first shipment of infected cherry trees that had been sent from Japan as well as the successful plantings around the Tidal Basin.

Head gardener Charles Henlock, just before his retirement from the White House in 1931, working in the propagating greenhouses near the Washington Monument.

William Saunders Reeves (1880–1946)

Served 1931–1945, under Herbert Hoover and Franklin Roosevelt.

William Saunders Reeves was the first American-born White House head gardener, hailing from Washington D.C. His grandfather, William Saunders (1822–1900), was the chief of the experimental gardens for the U.S. Department of Agriculture and founder of the National Grange but is perhaps best remembered for introducing the navel orange. According to census records, William S. Reeves lived with his grandfather, who no doubt trained him and influenced his choice of careers. Reeves worked under both Roosevelts, starting as an entry-level groundskeeper at the White House during the Theodore Roosevelt administration in 1903. Through World War I, he was gardener-shepherd to Wilson's flock of sheep. Reeves became head gardener and chief floral designer while Hoover was in office. In 1933, the National Park Service assumed responsibility for the White House grounds; thus Reeves transferred, and later head gardeners worked under its aegis. Eleanor Roosevelt found him delightful, not to mention trustworthy, writing, "His reticence was really remarkable."

Robert M. Redmond (1907–1976)

Served 1945–1962, under Harry Truman, Dwight Eisenhower, and John Kennedy.

Born in 1907, the tall, red-haired Robert Redmond started mowing lawns at the White House as a teenager during the Coolidge administration. "Red" climbed the ladder until, under Truman, he was made superintendent of the White House grounds. Redmond was the last head gardener at the White House also to be responsible for indoor floral decorations. Jacqueline Kennedy appointed Rusty Young, a designer with a more contemporary aesthetic, to the new post of chief floral designer in 1961.

Robert Redmond, the last head gardener to also be the chief florist, working on an arrangement of gladiolas, chrysanthemums, and roses in 1949.

Irvin Williams

Served 1962–2008, under John Kennedy, Lyndon Johnson, Richard Nixon, Gerald Ford, Jimmy Carter, Ronald Reagan, George H. W. Bush, Bill Clinton, and George W. Bush.

When Rachel "Bunny" Mellon and Perry Wheeler designed the Rose Garden for President Kennedy, they handpicked a horticulturist to supervise the installation. Irvin Williams had been a gardener with the National Park Service since 1949 when he was hired for the Kenilworth

"Gardening is my first love," said Irv Williams. The head gardener at the White House for forty-six years added, "It's the best profession in the world."

Aquatic Gardens. The son of a West Virginia farmer, Williams loved plants. He worked for the Park Service in various assignments, including the Baltimore-Washington Parkway and at the nurseries for the National Capital Region. When he transferred to the White House in 1962 he stayed on, supervising the work on the grounds for nine administrations. His co-workers often called the silver-haired Williams "Whitey."

Dale Haney

Served beginning in 2008, under George W. Bush and Barack Obama.

Like many of the White House head gardeners before him, Dale Haney was promoted from within. He started as a National Park Service gardener at the White House in 1972 after obtaining an associate's degree in horticulture from Sandhills Community College in Pinehurst, North Carolina. He has been a favorite with presidential canines over the years and is often photographed walking the current first dog. In 2008, he was appointed superintendent of the grounds.

All the Presidents' Plants

Two Centuries of Shrubs, Trees, and Vines

Tastes change in horticulture, and three White House inventories of woody plants grown on the grounds over the past two hundred years give a glimpse of the trends. The earliest list, from 1809, included close to 50 species of trees, shrubs, and vines. By 1900, the count had risen to more than 150 species, underscoring the eclectic sensibility typical to the period, as well as access to new plant imports. Conifers, magnolias, and flowering shrubs were especially popular. Fast-forward to the twenty-first century and woody plant diversity tapers off to just over 100 species, of which one-quarter include specimens planted prior to 1900.

A scant number of plants have been grown over the whole timespan: one shrub—the rose, that most charismatic of plants; one evergreen—the American holly; one European tree—the horse chestnut; and six trees native to eastern North America—the sugar maple, tulip poplar, and American ash, beech, elm, and redbud. Notably, the California redwood (*Sequoia sempervirens*) missed the list. Though gardeners planted one at the White House in 1906 during Teddy Roosevelt's administration and the Nixons planted another in 1971, neither survived. There are regional differences in American growing conditions that even a president's gardener cannot overcome.

The long tradition of tree planting at the White House was underscored on May 14, 1991, when President George H. W. Bush and Her Majesty the Queen planted a small-leaf linden to replace one that was blown down in a storm. Prince Philip looks on. (The original linden had been planted in 1937 to commemorate the coronation of Elizabeth II's father, King George VI.)

The introduction of plants now considered invasive began at the beginning, with bladder senna, and accelerated in the nineteenth century with plants like barberry and Norway maple. Today, plants on the invasive lists for the Washington D.C. area are not added to the White House grounds, though historic specimen trees such as paulownia are maintained.

COMMON NAME	BOTANICAL NAME	NATIVE?	1809	1900	2008
Shrubs					
althaea (rose of Sharon)	*Hibiscus syriacus*			❖	❖	
angelica, Chinese	*Aralia chinensis*			❖	
aucuba	*Aucuba japonica*			❖	
azalea, evergreen	*Rhododendron* ×			❖	❖
bamboo, arrow	*Pseudosasa japonica*			❖	
bamboo, golden	*Phyllostachys aurea*			❖	
barberry, hybrid	*Berberis* ×*gladwynensis*				❖
barberry, purple	*Berberis thunbergii* f. *atropurpurea*			❖	
bladder senna	*Colutea arborescens*		❖		
boxwood, American	*Buxus sempervirens*			❖	❖
boxwood, Japanese	*Buxus microphylla*				❖
boxwood, Korean	*Buxus sinica* var. *insularis*				❖
bridal wreath spiraea	*Spiraea cantoniensis*			❖	
broom, Scotch	*Cytisus scoparius*		❖		

ABOUT THE PLANT LIST

- Botanical names reflect current nomenclature.
- "Native" column refers to plants native to the lower 48 states.
- Each entry may represent one or more than one specimen on the grounds.
- White House inventory years are displayed in bold type, as shown below.

NOTES AND CULTIVARS

1809 listed red, white, double, and striped.

1900 listed as *Dimorphanthus mandschuricus.*

1900 listed cultivar 'Variegata'.

1900 listed as *Azalea amaena.* **2008** included the hybrid cultivars *R.* 'Blaauw's Pink', 'Delaware Valley White', 'Encore', 'Girard's Crimson', 'Kurume Snow', 'Pleasant White', 'Robin Hill Gillie', and 'White Indica'.

1900 listed as *Bambusa metake.*

1900 listed as Bambus (golden).

2008 listed cultivar 'William Penn'. This hybrid cultivar, developed by the Henry Foundation of Gladwyne, Pennsylvania, is sterile and thus non-invasive.

1900 listed as *B. purpurea* (purple leaved).

1900 listed tree and yellow-leaved forms as well as the straight species. **2008** listed the cultivars 'Suffruticosa', planted by Truman in front of the North Portico in 1952, and 'Vardar Valley'.

2008 listed cultivars 'Green Pillow', 'Kingsville Dwarf', and var. *japonica* 'Green Beauty'.

2008 listed cultivar 'Justin Brouwers'.

1900 listed as *S. reevesii* along with *S. reevesii flora plena.*

WHITE HOUSE INVENTORIES

1809 "Landscape Account for the Executive Mansion, 31 March 1809," Founders Online, National Archives. *The Papers of James Madison, Presidential Series, volume 1,* ed. Robert A. Rutland, et. al. (Charlottesville: University of Virginia Press, 1984), pp. 93–95.

1900 Inventory completed by head gardener Henry Pfister and submitted as part of *Annual Report Upon the Improvement and Care of Public Buildings and Grounds, Appendix HHH of the Annual Report of the Chief of Engineers for 1900* (Washington, D.C.: Government Printing Office, 1900), pp. 5245–5249.

2008 *The White House Gardens and Grounds: 2004–2008,* ed. Office of the National Park Service Liaison to the White House (Washington D.C.: White House Historical Association, one in a series published since 1976).

COMMON NAME	BOTANICAL NAME	NATIVE?	1809	1900	2008
Shrubs CONTINUED					
broom, Spanish	*Spartium junceum*		❖		
bush clover	*Lespedeza thunbergii*			❖	
California lilac	*Ceanothus*	❖		❖	
camellia	*Camellia japonica*				❖
crape myrtle	*Lagerstroemia* spp.			❖	❖
currant, golden	*Ribes aureum*	❖		❖	
deutzia	*Deutzia* spp.			❖	
euonymus, wintercreeper	*Euonymus fortunei*				❖
false indigo	*Amorpha fruticosa*			❖	
firethorn	*Pyracantha coccinea*				❖
forsythia	*Forsythia suspensa* var. *fortunei*			❖	
forsythia, greenstem	*Forsythia viridissima*				❖
forsythia, hybrid	*Forsythia ×intermedia*				❖
heavenly bamboo	*Nandina domestica*				❖
holly, littleleaf	*Ilex crenata*				❖
holly, winterberry	*Ilex verticillata*	❖		❖	
honeysuckle, bush	*Lonicera* spp.			❖	
honeysuckle, tatarian	*Lonicera tatarica*			❖	
hydrangea, mophead	*Hydrangea macrophylla*			❖	
hydrangea, panicled	*Hydrangea paniculata*			❖	
jasmine, winter	*Jasminum nudiflorum*			❖	
juniper	*Juniperus* spp.		❖	❖	
laurel	*Prunus laurocerasus*			❖	
lilac, common	*Syringa vulgaris*			❖	❖

NOTES AND CULTIVARS

1900 listed as *Desmodium japonicum* (white and purple varieties).

1900 listed as *C.* (gloir de plantier), possibly hybrid cultivar 'Gloire de Versailles'.

Gardeners grew camellias in the White House conservatories in the nineteenth century, but it took another fifty years before the first were planted outdoors in 1952. **2008** listed straight species, the hybrid *C.* × 'Survivor', and cultivars 'Brilliant', 'Tricolor Sieboldii', and 'Victory White'.

1900 listed *alba*, *purpurea*, *rosea*, and *violacea*. **2008** listed the hybrid cultivar *L.* × 'Potomac'.

1900 listed as *R. aureum* (Missouri currant). The golden currant was first identified from specimens collected by Meriwether Lewis in Montana in 1805.

1900 listed *D. gracilis* and *D. crenata*, as well as *D. crenata flora plena*.

2008 listed cultivar 'Colorata'.

2008 listed cultivar 'Lalandei'.

1900 listed as *Forsythia fortunii*.

2008 listed cultivar 'Spring Glory'.

2008 listed the cultivars 'Convexa', 'Microphylla', and 'Microphylla Glossy Leaf'.

1900 listed as *Prinos verticilatus* (black alder).

1900 listed cultivar 'Thomas Hogg'. Abraham Lincoln appointed Hogg U.S. Marshall to Japan in 1862. While there, Hogg studied and collected plants, including this white hydrangea.

1809 unknown variety, native assumed.

1809 and **1900** both listed purple and white.

COMMON NAME	BOTANICAL NAME	NATIVE?	1809	1900	2008
Shrubs CONTINUED					
lilac, Persian	Syringa ×persica		❖	❖	
mahonia, Japanese	Mahonia japonica			❖	
mock orange, double	Philadelphus coronarius			❖	
osmanthus, holly	Osmanthus heterophyllus				❖
pearlbush	Exochorda grandiflora			❖	
peony, tree	Paeonia suffruticosa				❖
privet	Ligustrum ovalifolium		❖	❖	
quince, Japanese	Chaenomeles japonica			❖	❖
rhododendron, catawba	Rhododendron catawbiense	❖			❖
rhododendron, hybrid	Rhododendron ×				❖
rose	Rosa spp.		❖	❖	❖
salt cedar, African	Tamarix africana			❖	
silverberry, fruitland	Eleagnus pungens				❖
smokebush	Cotinus coggygria			❖	
spirea, bridal wreath	Spiraea prunifolia			❖	
St. John's wort	Hypericum ×moserianum			❖	
St. John's wort, shrubby	Hypericum prolificum			❖	
sweetshrub	Calycanthus floridus	❖		❖	
thorn, evergreen	Crataegus spp.		❖		
viburnum	Viburnum spp.			❖	
viburnum, Chinese	Viburnum macrocephalum				❖
viburnum, doublefile	Viburnum plicatum f. tomentosum				❖
viburnum, Korean spice	Viburnum carlesii				❖
viburnum, snowball	Viburnum plicatum			❖	

NOTES AND CULTIVARS

1900 listed as California privet.

2008 listed cultivar 'Roseum Elegans'.

1809 listed "Roses," without naming species or cultivars. **1900** listed 'Empress of China' and *Rosa rugosa*. **2008** listed eleven varieties: the floribundas 'Iceberg', 'Laura Bush', and 'Pat Nixon'; the hybrid teas 'Barbara Bush', 'Nancy Reagan', 'Opening Night', 'Pope John Paul II', and 'Ronald Reagan'; and the hybrid musks 'Danae', 'Erfurt', and 'Francesa'. Rose selections are sometimes changed from administration to administration for obvious reasons.

2008 listed cultivar 'Fruitlandii'.

1900 listed as smoke tree.

2008 listed cultivar 'Sterile'.

2008 listed cultivar 'Mariesii'.

COMMON NAME	BOTANICAL NAME	NATIVE?	1809	1900	2008
Shrubs CONTINUED					
viburnum, southern blackhaw	*Viburnum rufidulum*	❖			❖
weigela	*Weigela florida*			❖	
winterhazel	*Corylopsis spicata*				❖
wintersweet	*Chimonanthus praecox*				❖
witch hazel, Japanese	*Hamamelis japonica*			❖	
yew, English	*Taxus baccata*			❖	❖
yew, hybrid	*Taxus ×media*				❖
yew, Japanese	*Taxus cuspidata*				❖
yucca	*Yucca filamentosa*	❖		❖	
Trees					
almond, double-flowering	*Prunus glandulosa* 'Plena'			❖	
Amur cork tree	*Phellodendron amurense*			❖	❖
apple, red delicious	*Malus pumila*				❖
arborvitae, American	*Thuja occidentalis*	❖		❖	
arborvitae, Japanese	*Thuja standishii*		❖	❖	
ash, American	*Fraxinus americana*	❖	❖	❖	❖
ash, English	*Fraxinus excelsior*			❖	
ash, green	*Fraxinus pennsylvanica ×angustifolia*	❖		❖	❖
ash, mountain	*Sorbus aucuparia*		❖	❖	
beech, American	*Fagus grandifolia*	❖	❖	❖	❖
beech, European	*Fagus sylvatica*			❖	❖
birch, European	*Betula pendula*			❖	
buckeye, red	*Aesculus pavia*	❖		❖	
buckeye, yellow	*Aesculus flava*	❖	❖	❖	
catalpa	*Catalpa bignonioides*	❖	❖	❖	

NOTES AND CULTIVARS

1900 listed both *W. rosea* and *W. folis variegatea*.

1900 listed cultivars 'Pyramidalis' and 'Washingtonii'. **2008** listed the Irish Yew as *T. baccata hibernica* 'Moon Columnaris'.

2008 listed cultivars 'Hatfieldii' and 'Hicksii'.

1900 listed as yuccas in a clump.

Could be *P. triloba*. **1900** classified it as a shrub.

1900 also listed the common name swamp cedar, and the cultivars 'Aurea', 'Filifera', 'Pyramidalis', 'Vervaeneana', and 'Wareana'.

1809 listed as Chinese arborvitae. **1900** listed as *Thujopsis standishii*.

Specific epithet not provided in **1809** or **1900**. **2008** listed as *F. americana*, then annotated as *F. pennsylvatica*. Cultivar 'Patmore' also listed in **2008**.

1900 listed as willow-leaved ash.

Noted as Rowentree (Rowan Tree) in **1809**.

Unspecified in **1809**, native assumed.

1900 and **2008** listed cultivars 'Asplenifolia' (cut-leaved), 'Atropunicea' (purple), and 'Riversii' (River's purple). **1900** also listed 'Purpurea Pendula' (weeping purple) and fern-leaved (now classified as 'Asplenifolia').

1900 listed as *B. alba* and also listed cultivar 'Dalecarlica' (cut-leaved weeping).

1900 also listed small-leaved, perhaps *A. glabra*.

Unspecified in **1809**, native assumed.

COMMON NAME	BOTANICAL NAME	NATIVE?	1809	1900	2008
Trees CONTINUED					
cedar of Lebanon	*Cedrus libani*				❖
cedar, atlas	*Cedrus atlantica*			❖	
cedar, blue atlas	*Cedrus atlantica* Glauca Group			❖	❖
cedar, California incense	*Calocedrus decurrens*	❖		❖	
cedar, deodar	*Cedrus deodara*			❖	
cherry, autumn higan	*Prunus subhirtella* 'Autumnalis'				❖
cherry, Japanese	*Prunus serrulata*			❖	
cherry, Japanese	*Prunus* ×*sieboldii*			❖	❖
cherry, sour	*Prunus cerasus*			❖	
cherry, sweet double-flowered	*Prunus avium*			❖	
cherry, weeping	*Prunus pendula*			❖	
cherry, wild	*Prunus serotina*	❖		❖	
cherry, Yoshino	*Prunus* ×*yedoensis*				❖
chestnut, Chinese	*Castanea mollissima*				❖
chestnut, Spanish	*Castanea sativa*			❖	
cornelian cherry	*Cornus mas*			❖	❖
crabapple	*Malus* cv.			❖	❖
crabapple, Japanese flowering	*Malus floribunda*				❖
crabapple, Parkman	*Malus halliana* var. *parkmanii*			❖	
crabapple, Siberian	*Malus baccata*			❖	
crabapple, tea	*Malus hupensis*				❖
cypress, bald	*Taxodium distichum*	❖		❖	❖
cypress, Lawson	*Chamaecyparis lawsonii*	❖		❖	
cypress, Leyland	×*Cuprocyparis leylandii*				❖
dogwood	*Cornus florida*	❖		❖	❖

NOTES AND CULTIVARS

2008 listed cultivar 'Argentea'.

1900 listed as *Libocedrus decurens*.

1900 listed as *C. deodara glauca*.

1900 also listed the double yellow-flowered Japanese cherry, probably the cultivar 'Ukon'.

1900 listed as *Cerasus sieboldii flora rosea plena*. **2008** listed hybrid cultivar 'Okame'

1900 listed as *Cerasus acida* (sour cherry).

1900 listed as *Cerasus avium alba plena*.

1900 listed as *Cerasus jap. rosea pendula* (weeping cherry).

2008 listed cultivars 'Brandywine', 'Katherine', and 'Mary Potter'.

1900 listed as *Pyrus malus parkmanni*.

1900 listed as Virginian cypress.

1900 listed as *Cupressus lawsoniana*.

1900 also listed *C. florida rubra* and *pendula*. **2008** listed cultivars 'Cherokee Princess', 'First Lady', and 'Ruth Ellen'.

COMMON NAME	BOTANICAL NAME	NATIVE?	1809	1900	2008
Trees CONTINUED					
dogwood, Korean	*Cornus kousa*				❖
elm, American	*Ulmus americana*	❖	❖	❖	❖
elm, Camperdown	*Ulmus glabra* 'Camperdownii'			❖	❖
elm, Chinese lacebark	*Ulmus parviflora*				❖
elm, English	*Ulmus procera*			❖	❖
elm, hybrid	*Ulmus wilsoniana* var. *japonica*				❖
empress tree	*Paulownia tomentosa*			❖	❖
epaulette tree	*Pterostyrax hispida*			❖	
filbert	*Corylus maxima*		❖		
fir, Douglas	*Pseudotsuga menziesii*	❖		❖	
fir, Greek	*Abies cephalonica*			❖	
fir, noble	*Abies procera*	❖		❖	
fir, Nordmann	*Abies nordmanniana*			❖	
fir, Pacific silver	*Abies amabilis*	❖		❖	
fir, Rocky Mountain	*Abies lasiocarpa*	❖		❖	
fir, silver	*Abies alba*			❖	
fir, Spanish	*Abies pinsapo*			❖	
fringe tree	*Chionanthus virginicus*	❖		❖	❖
ginkgo	*Ginkgo biloba*			❖	❖
golden chain	*Laburnum anagyroides*		❖	❖	
goldenrain tree	*Koelreuteria paniculata*			❖	
gum, black	*Nyssa sylvatica*	❖			❖
hawthorn	*Crataegus viridis*				❖
hemlock	*Tsuga canadensis*	❖	❖	❖	
holly, American	*Ilex opaca*	❖	❖	❖	❖
holly, Chinese	*Ilex cornuta*			❖	❖

NOTES AND CULTIVARS

2008 listed cultivar 'Centennial'.

Unspecified in **1809**, native assumed. **2008** listed cultivars 'Horace Westor', 'Jefferson', and 'Washington'.

1900 listed as *Ulmus pendula camperdownii*.

Note that this species is named for Ernest Wilson, Scottish-American plant collector, not President Wilson. **2008** listed both this and an unspecified hybrid.

1900 listed as *Paulownia imperialis.*

1900 listed as *Halesia hispida.*

1900 listed as *Abies douglasii.*

1900 listed as *Picea cephalonica.*

1900 listed as *Abies nobilis.*

1900 listed as *Picea nordmanniana.*

1900 listed as *A. canadensis compacta glauca.*

1900 listed as *Abies pectinata.*

Listed by **1900** as *Salisburia adiantifolia.*

1900 listed as *Cytisus laburnum* (golden chain).

2008 listed cultivar 'Winter King'.

1809, species not given, native assumed. **1900** listed as *Abies canadensis* (hemlock).

1809, species not given, native assumed. In **2008**, specimens included the topiary grown in the Jacqueline Kennedy garden and the cultivars 'Miss Helen' and 'Xanthocarpa' (yellow-fruited).

COMMON NAME	BOTANICAL NAME	NATIVE?	1809	1900	2008
Trees CONTINUED					
holly, English	*Ilex aquifolium*		❖	❖	❖
holly, hybrid	*Ilex* ×				❖
holly, lusterleaf	*Ilex latifolia*				❖
honey locust	*Gleditsia tricanthos*	❖	❖		
honey locust, Chinese	*Gleditsia sinensis*			❖	
hop tree, golden	*Ptelea trifoliata* 'Aurea'			❖	
hornbeam, European	*Carpinus betulus*			❖	
horse chestnut	*Aesculus hippocastanum*		❖	❖	❖
Judas tree	*Cercis siliquastrum*			❖	
katsura	*Cercidiphyllum japonicum*				❖
larch	*Larix laricina*	❖	❖		
larch, European	*Larix decidua*			❖	
lilac, tree	*Syringa reticulata*			❖	❖
linden, American	*Tilia americana*	❖		❖	
linden, European	*Tilia platyphyllos*			❖	❖
linden, little leaf	*Tilia cordata*				❖
linden, silver	*Tilia tomentosa*				❖
linden, weeping silver	*Tilia tomentosa* 'Petiolaris'			❖	❖
locust, common	*Robinia pseudoacacia*	❖	❖	❖	
locust, scarlet	*Sesbania punicea*			❖	
magnolia, bigleaf	*Magnolia macrophylla*	❖		❖	
magnolia, kobus	*Magnolia kobus*				❖
magnolia, lily-flowering	*Magnolia quinquepeta*			❖	❖
magnolia, Loebner	*Magnolia* ×*loebneri* 'Merrill'				❖
magnolia, saucer	*Magnolia* ×*soulangeana*			❖	
magnolia, southern	*Magnolia grandiflora*	❖		❖	❖

NOTES AND CULTIVARS

1900 listed as *Ilex aquifolia* (European holly).

2008 listed hybrid cultivars 'Emily Brunner', 'Nellie R. Stevens', 'Oakleaf', 'Wye River Queen', and ×*altaclarensis*, *altaclarensis* 'Camelliifolia', *I. attenuata* 'East Palatka', ×*attenuata* 'Fosteri', and ×*koehneana*.

1900 also listed *A. hippocastanum* 'Baumannii'.

1900 listed as Japanese red bud (Judas tree).

1900 listed *S. Ligustrina* and *japonica*, now combined.

1900 listed common name only.

1900 listed as *M. purpurata*.

1900 also listed *M. soulangeana* 'Lennei'. **2008** also listed 'Alba'.

1900 also listed the cultivar *M. grandiflora* 'Galissonière'.

COMMON NAME	BOTANICAL NAME	NATIVE?	1809	1900	2008
Trees CONTINUED					
magnolia, star	*Magnolia stellata*			❖	❖
magnolia, sweetbay	*Magnolia virginiana*	❖		❖	
magnolia, Yulan	*Magnolia denudata*				❖
mahogany, Chinese	*Toona sinensis*			❖	
maple, Amur	*Acer tataricum* ssp. *ginnala*			❖	
maple, ash-leaved	*Acer negundo*			❖	
maple, cut-leaved	*Acer saccharinum*	❖		❖	❖
maple, field	*Acer campestre*			❖	
maple, Japanese	*Acer palmatum*			❖	❖
maple, Norway	*Acer platanoides*			❖	
maple, red	*Acer rubrum*	❖		❖	❖
maple, sugar	*Acer saccharum*	❖	❖	❖	❖
mimosa	*Albizia julibrissin*			❖	
mulberry, Chinese	*Morus alba*		❖		
mulberry, English	*Morus nigra*		❖		
oak, black	*Quercus velutina*	❖		❖	
oak, bur	*Quercus macrocarpa*	❖		?	❖
oak, chestnut	*Quercus montana*	❖		❖	❖
oak, cork	*Quercus suber*			❖	
oak, golden	*Quercus robur* 'Concordia'			❖	
oak, Japanese emperor	*Quercus dentata*			❖	
oak, large-leaved	*Quercus castanea* var. *macrophylla*	❖		❖	
oak, laurel-leaved	*Quercus hemisphaerica*	❖		❖	
oak, pin	*Quercus palustris*	❖		❖	❖
oak, red	*Quercus rubra*	❖		❖	❖

NOTES AND CULTIVARS

1900 listed as *M. halleana*.

1900 listed as *M. glauca*.

1900 listed as *Cedrella sinensis*.

1900 and **2008** listed cultivar 'Wieri'.

1900 also listed both *purpureum* and *atropurpureum*. **2008** listed 'Bloodgood' and 'Tsukabane'. **1900** and **2008** both listed cultivar 'Dissectum' (threadleaf).

1900 also listed *A. ritenbachi A. platanoides* 'Schwedleri', and separately listed sycamore maple.

1900 also listed scarlet and swamp maples. **2008** also listed cultivar 'October Glory'.

1900 listed as *Acacia nemu*.

The inclusion of the white mulberry reflects an early interest in silk culture, as the leaves of this species are the preferred food of silkworms. John Quincy and Louisa Adams raised silkworms at the White House.

Not listed in **1900**; in **2008** listed as planted pre-**1900**.

1900 listed as olive oak.

1900 also listed European oak, unspecified.

1900 listed as *Q. concordia*.

1900 listed as Japanese oak (Daimio).

1900 listed as *Q. macrophylla*.

Q. borealis listed separately in **1900** and **2008**, now combined.

COMMON NAME	BOTANICAL NAME	NATIVE?	1809	1900	2008
Trees CONTINUED					
oak, scarlet	Quercus coccinea	❖		❖	❖
oak, swamp white	Quercus bicolor	❖		❖	❖
oak, white	Quercus alba	❖		❖	❖
oak, willow	Quercus phellos	❖	❖		❖
orange, hardy	Poncirus trifoliata			❖	❖
pagoda tree, Japanese	Styphnolobium japonicum			❖	❖
parrotia, Persian	Parrotia persica			?	❖
peach, double-flowering	Prunus persica		❖	❖	
persimmon, European	Diospyros lotus			❖	
pine, Austrian	Pinus nigra			❖	
pine, Himalayan	Pinus wallichiana			❖	
pine, Korean	Pinus koraiensis			❖	
pine, loblolly	Pinus taeda	❖			❖
pine, Scotch	Pinus sylvestris			❖	
pine, Swiss mountain	Pinus cembra			❖	
pine, white	Pinus strobus	❖	❖	❖	
plum, purple-leaved	Prunus cerasifera 'Pissardii'			❖	
poplar, silver leaf	Populus alba			❖	
redbud	Cercis canadensis	❖	❖	❖	❖
silverbell	Halesia tetraptera	❖		❖	
snowbell, Japanese	Styrax japonicus			❖	
sorrel tree	Oxydendrum arboreum	❖		❖	
spruce	Picea spp.		❖		
spruce, Colorado	Picea pungens	❖		❖	
spruce, Norway	Picea abies			❖	
spruce, Oriental	Picea orientalis			❖	❖
spruce, tigertail	Picea torano			❖	
sweetgum	Liquidambar styraciflua	❖		❖	

1900 listed as large-leaved white oak.

1900 listed as *Limonia trifoliata*.

1900 listed as *Sophora japonica* (Japanese varnish tree).

Not listed in **1900**; in **2008** listed as planted pre-**1900**.

1900 listed double red- and white-flowered. The double-flowered cultivar is 'Plena'.

1900 listed as *P. austriaca*.

1900 listed as *P. excela*.

1900 listed as *P. coracensis* (Corean pine).

1900 listed as *P. scoticus*.

1900 listed as *P. cembra compacta*.

1900 also listed *P. strobus compactus nanus*.

1900 listed as *P. pissardii*.

In **1809**, unspecified and the native assumed. **2008** also listed cultivar 'Alba'.

1900 listed as *Andromeda arborea*.

Unspecified in **1809**.

1900 listed as *Abies pungens*.

1900 listed as *Abies excelsa*.

1900 listed as *Abies*; ssp. *compacta* also included.

1900 listed as *Abies polita*.

COMMON NAME	BOTANICAL NAME	NATIVE?	1809	1900	2008
Trees CONTINUED					
sycamore, American	*Platanus occidentalis*	❖		❖	❖
sycamore, English	*Platanus ×acerifolia*		❖		❖
sycamore, Oriental	*Platanus orientalis*			❖	
tulip poplar	*Liriodendron tulipifera*	❖	❖	❖	❖
walnut, black	*Juglans nigra*	❖		❖	
walnut, English	*Juglans regia*		❖		
willow, golden	*Salix alba* 'Vitellina'			❖	
willow, Russian	*Salix alba*			❖	
willow, weeping	*Salix babylonica*		❖		
yellowwood	*Cladrastis kentukea*	❖		❖	❖
Vines					
clematis	*Clematis* spp.			❖	
clematis, sweet autumn	*Clematis paniculata*			❖	
grape, Concord	*Vitis labrusca* 'Concord'				❖
honeysuckle, early	*Lonicera periclymenum*		❖		
honeysuckle, Hall's	*Lonicera japonica* 'Halliana'			❖	
honeysuckle, monthly	*Lonicera* spp.		❖		
honeysuckle, trumpet	*Lonicera sempervirens*	❖	❖	❖	
ivy, English	*Hedera helix*				❖
jasmine, white	*Jasminum officinale*		❖		
jasmine, yellow	*Lonicera flava*	❖	❖		
trumpet vine	*Bignonia grandiflora*	❖	❖	❖	
wisteria, Chinese	*Wisteria sinensis*			❖	❖
wisteria, Japanese white	*Wisteria floribunda* 'Alba'			❖	
COUNT			46	169	102

NOTES AND CULTIVARS

1900 listed as tulip tree, and separately listed the variegated cultivar, 'Aureo-marginatum'.

1900 listed as *Virgilia lutea* (yellow wood).

1900 listed "Clematis and roses."

1900 listed as *Lonicera halleana*.

1900 listed as red-flowered honeysuckle.

2008 also listed the cultivar 'Needlepoint', planted in 1990. Needlepoint was a favorite hobby of First Lady Barbara Bush.

1900 spelled the genus *Wistaria*.

1900 listed as *Wistaria japonica*.

Recommended Reading

The White House and Its Gardens Through the Years

Boyle, Susan Calafate, et al. *The White House & President's Park Cultural Landscape Report: Site History and Evaluation: 1791–1994* (Washington D.C.: National Park Service, 2001).

Dietz, Ulysses Grant, and Sam Watters. *Dream House* (New York: Acanthus Press, 2009).

Garrett, William, ed. *Our Changing White House* (Boston: Northeastern University Press, 1995), includes Susanne Turner's essay "The Landscape of the President's House: Garden of Democracy."

Guidas, John. *The White House: Resources for Research at the Library of Congress* (Washington D.C.: Library of Congress, 1992).

Holden, Linda Hoyt. *Presidents' Gardens* (Long Island City, NY: Shire Publications, 2013).

Kramer, Frederick L., ed. *The White House Gardens: A History and Pictorial Record* (New York: Great American Editions, 1973).

McEwan, Barbara. *White House Landscapes: Horticultural Achievements of the American Presidents* (New York: Walker & Co. 1992).

Monkman, Betty C. *The White House: Its Historic Furnishings and First Families* (New York: Abbeville Press, 2000).

Seale, William. *The President's House* (Washington D.C.: White House Historical Association, 2008).

———. *White House Gardens* (Washington D.C.: White House Historical Association, 1996).

White House History, the magazine that William Seale edits for the White House Historical Association.

The History of American Gardening

Adams, Denise Wiles. *Restoring American Gardens: An Encyclopedia of Heirloom Ornamental Plants, 1640–1940* (Portland, OR: Timber Press, 2004).

Adams, Denise Wiles, and Laura L. S. Burchfield. *American Home Landscapes: A Design Guide to Creating Period Garden Styles* (Portland, OR: Timber Press, 2013).

Favretti, Jody, and Rudy Favretti. *Landscapes and Gardens for Historic Buildings* (Lanham, MD: Rowman Altamira Press, 1997).

Graham, Wade. *American Eden: From Monticello to Central Park to Our Backyards* (New York: HarperCollins, 2011).

Lacy, Allen, ed. *The American Gardener: A Sampler* (New York: Farrar Straus Giroux, 1988).

Leighton, Ann. *Early American Gardens: For Meate or Medicine* (Amherst: University of Massachusetts Press, 1970).

———. *American Gardens of the Eighteenth Century: For Use or For Delight* (Amherst: University of Massachusetts Press, 1976).

———. *American Gardens of the Nineteenth Century: For Comfort and Affluence.* (Amherst: University of Massachusetts Press, 1987).

Lockwood, Alice G. B., ed. *Gardens of Colony and State: Gardens and Gardeners of the American Colonies and of the Republic before 1840* (New York: Garden Club of America, 2000). See especially the description of Mount Vernon (volume 1: 55–65) and The Woodlands (volume 2: 346–350).

McGuire, Diane Kostial, ed. *American Garden Design: An Anthology of Ideas that Shaped Our Landscape* (New York: MacMillan, 1994).

O'Malley, Therese. *Keywords in American Landscape Design* (New Haven, CT: Yale University Press, 2010).

Punch, Walter T., ed. *Keeping Eden: A History of Gardening in America* (Boston: Massachusetts Horticultural Society, 1992).

Rogers, Elizabeth Barlow. *Landscape Design: A Cultural and Architectural History* (New York: Harry N. Abrams, 2001).

Stiloge, John R. *Common Landscape of America, 1580–1845* (New Haven, CT: Yale University Press, 1983).

Watts, May Theilgaard. *Reading the Landscape of America* (New York: Macmillan, 1975).

Sources and Citations

Prologue

Because the agricultural practices of the original inhabitants of North America occurred before the written record, one relies on the observations of European explorers, some of whom were prone to exaggerate. One of those was John Smith, whose journal of his Potomac expedition of June 18–July 15, 1608, is transcribed at johnsmith400.org/history.htm.

Recent scholarship may be found in:

- Cronin, William. *Changes in the Land* (New York: Hill and Wang, 2003).
- Pierre, Catherine. "Stories from the Sediment," *Johns Hopkins Magazine* (February 2004).
- Smith, Bruce D. *Rivers of Change: Essays on Early Agriculture in Eastern North America* (Tuskaloosa: The University of Alabama Press, 2007).

Versailles on the Potomac

Online resources are deep and rich for the early national period. The National Archives, along with the Princeton University Press and the University of Virginia Press, provides web access to a treasure trove of primary sources from Washington and his cohort at Founders Online (founders. archives.gov). It is the source of the letters from:

- Pierre Charles L'Enfant to George Washington.
- Thomas Jefferson to Pierre Charles L'Enfant.
- George Washington to Thomas Jefferson (the source of "the obstinate Mr. Burns"), William Thornton (the source of "by the obstructions"), Oliver Wolcott Jr. (the source of "under my own Vine"), and Arthur Young.
- George Augustine Washington to George Washington.

Founders Online is also the source for:

- "To the memory" from the New-York Journal (August 31, 1790), cited in the editorial note, "Fixing the Seat of Government on the Potomac."
- George Washington's visit to Bartram's nursery, *Diaries 5* (June 1787), pp. 166–167.
- Bartram's 1792 plant list from Washington's papers.

The Library of Congress has tools (www.loc.gov/rr/program/bib/ourdocs/ Residence.html) including a virtual vertical file on the Residence Act; the quote "a pill peculiarly" is available in the introduction to the "Anas," February 4, 1818. Its "American Memory" collection offers both facsimile and transcription of the Land Ordinance of 1785, authored by Jefferson and his committee.

Bowling, Kenneth R. *The Creation of Washington D.C.* (Fairfax, VA: George Mason University Press, 1991).

———. *Peter Charles L'Enfant: Vision, Honor and Male Friendship in the Early American Republic* (Washington D.C.: Friends of George Washington University, 2002).

Busey, Samuel Clagett. *Pictures of the City of Washington in the Past* (Washington D.C.: W. Ballantyne & Sons, 1898). The quote "with punch and Madeira" is on p. 22.

Chernow, Ron. *Washington: A Life* (New York: Penguin Press, 2010). The quote "With me it" is on p. 4; the quote "raised the value" from John Adams is on p. 631.

Cothran, James R. *Gardens and Historic Plants of the Antebellum South* (Columbia: University of South Carolina Press, 2003).

Griswold, Mac. *Washington's Gardens at Mount Vernon* (New York: Houghton Mifflin, 1999).

Latrobe, Benjamin Henry. *The Journal of Latrobe, 1796 to 1820* (New York: D. Appleton and Company, 1905). The quote about Mount Vernon's garden is on p. 52.

Leone, Mark. *The Archaeology of Liberty in an American Capital: Excavation in Annapolis* (Los Angeles: University of California Press, 2005). The archaeological digs at Bacon's Castle in Virginia have overturned the Middleton Place's claim of America's first landscaped garden, but it remains a fine example of a falls garden.

Sarudy, Barbara Wells. *Gardens and Gardening in the Chesapeake, 1700–1805* (Baltimore: The Johns Hopkins University Press, 1998).

Wulf, Andrea. *Founding Gardeners* (New York: Knopf, 2011).

Founders' Grounds

Founders Online is the source of Jefferson's 1786 "Notes of a Tour of English Gardens"; Franklin's 1743 "Proposal for Promoting Useful Knowledge"; and the letters from:

- Thomas Jefferson to William Hamilton (source of "My green house"), Martha Jefferson Randolph, and Madame de Tessé.
- Benjamin Latrobe to Thomas Jefferson (source of "rendering the President's").
- Bernard McMahon to Thomas Jefferson.

The Massachusetts Historical Society provides access via www.masshist.org to the Adams Family Papers Electronic Archives. It is the source of the John Adams diary entries and the letters from:

- Abigail Adams to Elizabeth Cranch.
- John Adams to Abigail Adams.
- Lucy Cranch to Abigail Adams.

Monticello's online Jefferson Encyclopedia at www.monticello.org is the source for the information about Jefferson's interest in mockingbirds.

Adams, Abigail. *Letters of Mrs. Adams* (Boston: Charles C. Little and James Brown, 1840). The letter from Abigail Adams to Abigail Adams Smith (November 21, 1800) is the source of the quotes "We have not," "Woods are all," "Very many of," "grand and superb," and "It is a beautiful," pp. 433–435.

Adams, Henry. *The Life of Albert Gallatin* (Philadelphia: J. B Lippincott & C., 1879). The quote "swamp intervenes" is from a letter to his wife on January 15, 1801, pp. 252–253.

Dunlap, William. *Diary of William Dunlap: 1766–1839* (New York: New York Historical Society, 1932). The quote "He converses" is from volume 2, p. 388, February 25, 1806.

Ellis, Joseph. *First Family: Abigail and John Adams* (New York: Knopf, 2010). Abigail Adams's comparison of her husband to Jefferson is on p. 181.

Hatch, Peter J. *A Rich Spot of Earth: Thomas Jefferson's Revolutionary Garden at Monticello* (New Haven, CT: Yale University Press, 2014).

Jefferson, Thomas. *Thomas Jefferson's Garden Book*. Ed. Edwin Morris Betts (Charlottesville, VA: Thomas Jefferson Foundation, 2001).

Martin, Tovah. *Once Upon a Windowsill: A History of Indoor Plants* (Portland, OR: Timber Press, 1988).

McCullough, David. *John Adams* (New York: Simon & Schuster, 2001).

McMahon, Bernard. *McMahon's American Gardener* (New York: Funk & Wagnalls, 1976; reprint of the 11th edition, 1857). The 1857 edition includes a biographical essay about the author.

Meacham, Jon. *Thomas Jefferson: The Art of Power* (New York: Random House, 2012).

Smith, Margaret Bayard. *The First Forty Years of Washington Society* (New York: Charles Scribner's Sons, 1906). The quote "peculiar fondness" is on p. 385; "republican simplicity" pp. 391–392.

Watters, Sam. "Garden of Democracy," *Huntington Frontiers* (Spring/
Summer 2010), 24–26. This is the source of the William Thornton quotation "Avoid palaces."

Whately, Thomas. *Observations on Modern Gardening* (London: T. Payne
and Sons, 1777). The quote "But ground is seldom" is from p. 15; "naked and
neglected," "the appendages incidental," and "some degree of" are on pp.
176–177. Thanks to Open Library's archive.org, one may view online John
Adams's personal copy of Whately, complete with his notations, from the
collection of the Boston Public Library.

"The White House Fence Historic Timeline Overview," *The White House
Historical Association* (September 2014), pp. 1–3.

Gentlemen's Occupation

Founders Online is the source of the 1809 inventory of plants on the grounds
of the executive mansion and letters from James Madison to Benjamin
Latrobe and Elkanah Watson to James Madison. Note that Founders Online
ends with James Madison.

The Library of Congress online resources includes the letter from Bernard
McMahon to Benjamin Latrobe, June 27, 1809, with the seed order and the
quotes "I take the" and "P S. The Box."

The Massachusetts Historical Society's website provides facsimile images
of the fifty-one volumes of the diary of John Quincy Adams and is the
source of the excerpts and information about his growing interests. See
especially December 31, 1825, May–July 1827, and April–June 1828. Other
diary materials including the two botanical drawings included in this
chapter are only available at the reading room of the Society in Boston.

The University of Virginia Press, via Rotunda, provides *The Dolley Madison Digital Edition* including the letter from Dolley Madison to Phoebe
Morris, October 6, 1811.

For nineteenth-century books now in the public domain, resources like archive.org and Google Books provide easy access to authors such as Paul Jennings and Susan Fenimore Cooper.

Adams, William R. "The Live Oak Farm of John Quincy Adams," *Florida Historical Quarterly* (October 1972). Adams includes the letter from John Quincy Adams to George Adams.

Allgor, Catherine. *A Perfect Union: Dolley Madison and the Creation of an American Nation* (New York: Henry Holt & Company, 2006). Allgor cites *The Baltimore Whig* using "the white house" in 1810 on p. 171.

Ammon, Harry. *James Monroe: The Quest for National Identity* (Charlottesville: University of Virginia Press, 1990). The quote from Thomas Law, "When I perceive," is on p. 289.

"Columbian Horticultural Society, Washington, At the Fall Exhibition, November 7, 1835," *The American Gardener's Magazine* (December 1836), pp. 458–459, records Ousley's prizes.

Child, Lydia Maria. *The Mother's Book* (Boston: I. R. Butts, 1831). The quotations about the design of burial grounds are on p. 81.

Cooper, James Fenimore. *Notions of the Americans: Picked up by a Travelling Bachelor* (Philadelphia: Carey, Lea & Carey, 1832). The descriptions of the White House and the city are on pp. 20–22.

Dodenhoff, Donna. "The View from Montpelier," *Journal of the New England Garden History Society* (2001), pp. 1–10.

Eliot, Charles William. *Charles Eliot: Landscape Architect* (New York: Houghton, Mifflin and Company, 1902). The description of Gore Place is on p. 243.

Gardiner, John, and David Hepburn. *The American Gardener* (Washington D.C.: William Cooper, 1826). The list of tender annual flowers is on p. 174.

Grimsted, David. *American Mobbing: 1828–1861: Toward the Civil War* (New York: Oxford University Press, 1998). Information about the "professor" Adams and the "plowman" Jackson is on pp. 4–5.

Hatch, Peter J. *The Fruits and Fruit Trees of Monticello* (Charlottesville, VA: The Thomas Jefferson Foundation, 1998).

Jennings, Paul. *A Colored Man's Reminiscences of James Madison* (Brooklyn: George C. Beadle, 1865). The quote about Magraw the gardener is on p. 13.

Levasseur, Auguste. *Lafayette in America* (New York: White, Gallaher & White, 1829). The quote from Lafayette's secretary, "The land in," is on p. 56.

Mapes, James J. "Usefulness of the Arts of Design," *Sartain's Union Magazine of Literature and Art* 8 (1851), p. 252, including the quotation about Paulus Hedl.

"Matters at Washington," July 24, 1824 *Niles' Weekly Register* p. 340 is the source of the quote "see for himself," written by the mayor of Baltimore to the city council in advance of Lafayette's visit.

Mickey, Thomas J. *America's Romance with the English Garden* (Athens: Ohio University Press, 2013).

Miller, M. Stephen. *From Shaker Lands and Shaker Hands* (Lebanon, NH: University of New England Press, 2007).

Monroe, James. *The Papers of James Monroe: Volume I.* Ed. Daniel Preston (Westport, CT: Greenwood Press, 2003). The quotation from the *Boston Patriot* (July 7, 1817) about the garden visits in Waltham is on p. 227.

Shepherd, Jack. "Seeds of the Presidency," *Horticulture* (January 1963), pp. 38–47.

Turnbull, Martha. *The Garden Diary of Martha Turnbull, Mistress of Rosedown Plantation.* Ed. Suzanne Turner (Baton Rouge: Louisiana State University Press, 2012).

Embellishments

The National Archives and Records Administration (NARA) is the keeper of official files related to the White House grounds. Record Group 42 includes the majority of files related to the White House, such as the 1880 ledger book with details of personnel, hours, and tasks, including "abating nuisances," in the greenhouses and gardens. Andrew Jackson Downing's plan for the National Mall, including the president's house, is in Record Group 77 and available online at research.archives.gov; a facsimile of Downing's explanatory notes is included in Kramer's *The White House Gardens*.

The University of Michigan, through the efforts of the Abraham Lincoln Association, provides online access to *The Collected Works of Abraham Lincoln* (New Brunswick, NJ: Rutgers University Press, 1953) with full-text search capabilities. It is the source of his August 22, 1864, speech to the 166th Ohio Regiment.

The Poetry Foundation, via poetryfoundation.org, is the source of the excerpt from the Walt Whitman poem, "When Lilacs Last in the Dooryard Bloom'd."

Google Books is particularly helpful in sourcing reports from government agencies, such as the *Report of the Secretary of War to the U.S. House of Representatives* (Washington D.C.: Government Printing Office, 1869). This includes the report of the chief engineer responsible for public buildings and, on p. 501, the description of President Grant's billiard room and grapery at the White House.

Many newspapers from 1836 to 1922 are accessible via the Library of Congress Chronicling America site (chroniclingamerica.loc.gov). These include the Washington D.C. *Evening Star*, the source of information about John Watt in the 1850s. See:
- "A Delightful Half Hour," November 21, 1854, p. 3.
- "The Horticultural Exhibition," June 16, 1857, p. 3.
- "Washington Horticultural Society," September 21, 1857, p. 2.
- "The Executive Conservatory," October 2, 1858, p. 3.

Aniśko, Tomasz. *Victoria the Seductress* (Kennett Square, PA: Longwood Gardens, 2013). This beautiful volume about the history of the giant water lily is the source of the quote about the degradation of the conservatories during the tenure of John Watt, p. 188, cited as *Gardener's Monthly and Horticultural Advertiser* (1860), pp. 175–176.

Bayne, Julia Taft. *Tad Lincoln's Father* (Boston: Little, Brown, and Company, 1931). Taft's memories of John Watt, and the quotes "the bouquet man" and "He would take," are on p. 82.

Boller, Paul F. *Presidential Anecdotes* (New York: Oxford University Press, 1996). Secretary of State William Evarts's quote about the beverages served at the Hayes White House is on p. 165.

Crook, William H. *Through Five Administrations: Reminiscences of Colonel William H. Crook, Body-Guard to President Lincoln*. Ed. Margarita Spalding Gerry (New York: Harper & Brothers, 1910). The quote "The White House and its surroundings" is on p. 16.

Darrin, Charles V. "Your Truly Attached Friend, Mary Lincoln," *Journal of the Illinois State Historical Society* (Spring 1951), pp. 7–24. The letter from Mary Lincoln to Hannah Shearer is on p. 22.

Dickinson, Emily. *The Letters of Emily Dickinson*. Ed. Thomas H. Johnson (Cambridge, MA: Harvard University Press, 1986). The letter to Mrs. J. G. Holland is on p. 449.

Downing, Andrew Jackson. *Andrew Jackson Downing: Essential Texts*. Ed. Robert Twombly (New York: W. W. Norton & Company, 2012). This compilation is the source of quotations from Downing, taken from issues of *The Horticulturist* in the 1840s and 1850s and from the first edition of *A Treatise on the Theory and Practice of Landscape Gardening*.

———. *Landscape Gardening and Rural Architecture* (New York: Dover Publications, 1961; reprint of the 7th edition, 1865).

Epstein, Daniel Mark. *The Lincolns: Portrait of a Marriage* (New York: Random House, 2008). The description of John Watt as a "snake in the garden" with a "Manure Fund" is on p. 346.

"Gardening at the White House Fifty Years Ago," *Gardening* (September 15, 1905), pp. 2–3. Former head gardener Alexander McKerichar recording his memories of the White House gardens from the 1850s through the 1870s.

Keckley, Elizabeth. *Thirty Years a Slave, and Four Years in the White*

House (New York: G. W. Carleton & Co., 1868). The poet's description of Willie Lincoln as "a wild flower" is on p. 107.

Keeler, Lucy Elliot. *The Spiegel Grove State Park, the Hayes Memorial Museum, and the Hayes Homestead* (Fremont: The Ohio State Archaeological and Historical Society, 1926). A description of the historic trees planted at Spiegel Grove is included on p. 27.

McPeck, Eleanor M. *The President's Garden: An Account of the White House Gardens from 1800 to the Present* (Unpublished manuscript, 1971). Available at the Frances Loeb Library of the Harvard Graduate School of Design. The description of Miss Lane's conservatory from Frank Leslie's 1858 newspaper is on p. 31, including the quote "a most fitting."

Ogle, Charles. *Remarks of Mr. Ogle, of Pennsylvania, on the Civil and Diplomatic Appropriations Bill* (Washington D.C.: Government Printing Office, 1840). Called "the Gold Spoon Oration," this is the source of "an Amazon's Bosom," p. 5.

Pendel, Thomas F. *Thirty-Six Years in the White House* (Washington, D.C.: The Neale Publishing Company, 1902).

"Plants in Bloom at the White House, Washington," *Gardening* (March 15, 1894), p. 212 is the source for the quotation about Henry Pfister's amaryllis.

Whitman, Walt. *Memoranda During the War.* Ed. Peter Coviello (New York: Oxford University Press, 2004, originally published in 1875). The 1863 description of the White House at night is on pp. 11–12; the levee at the Lincoln White House is described on pp. 76–77.

Winkle, Kenneth J. *Lincoln's Citadel: The Civil War in Washington, D.C* (New York: W. W. Norton & Company, 2013).

Willets, Gilson. *Inside the White House* (New York: The Christian Herald, 1908). The description of Mrs. Grant's White House as "a garden spot of orchids" is on p. 138.

Gilded Gardens

In addition to Chronicling America at the Library of Congress, other newspaper collections from around the country are available in digital form, on the commercial subscription services Newpapers.com and ProQuest, and via publication-specific websites. Google Books also makes many old and unusual periodicals available to anyone with an Internet connection. These databases provided:

Bache, René. "Aquatic Gardening for Amateurs," *The Saturday Evening Post* (April 28, 1900), p. 1000, on water gardening in the United States and at the White House.

Blanchan, Neltje. "The Naturalistic Garden," *Country Life in America* (September 1908), pp. 443–444, with its description of carpet bedding as "pimples," "stereotyped beds," "prim rows," and "screaming scarlet geraniums."

Lester, M. H. "Public Gardens in Washington," *The Gardener's Monthly* (April 1887), p. 123, about the cutting flowers grown by Pfister.

"Floriculture at the White House," *American Florist* (October 1, 1888), p. 81, on Pfister's propagation and potting techniques, as well as the crotons in his carpet bedding.

Hatfield, T. D. "The Cultivation of Cannas," *Garden and Forest* (September 29, 1897), p. 384, on *Canna* 'President Cleveland'.

"In Uncle Sam's Nursery," *The Sunday Star*, Washington D.C. (April 30, 1905), p. 5, describes the transition of the White House propagation to the Monument grounds, along with the new responsibilities of George Hay Brown.

"More Garden Plans for the White House," *American Gardening* (June 27, 1903), p. 305, is the source of the *Washington Post* quote on the colonial garden of the White House, with plants including the golden rod.

Nehrling, H. "The Hippeastrums," *Garden and Forest* (May 19, 1897), pp. 194–195, with the discussion of Pfister's amaryllis hybrids, including cultivars named for Frances Cleveland and her daughters.

Oliver, G. W. "Plants in Bloom at the White House, Washington," *Gardening* (March 15, 1894), p. 212, on the crocuses and snowdrops in a wild garden design on the lawn.

———. "A New Bedding Plant, Strobilanthes Dyerianus," *American Gardening* (1894), p. 373, describes Pfister testing this new introduction at the White House gardens.

Pfister, Henry. "The Pampas-Grass in Washington, D.C.," *American Gardening* (1891), p. 758.

"Plant Labels," *Garden and Forest* (October 13, 1897), pp. 406–407, on Pfister's permanent greenhouse labels.

"Relic Hunters Haunt the White House," *The New York Times* (June 23, 1902), p. 3, on the removal of the greenhouses.

Smalley, E. V. "The White House," *The Century* (April 1884), pp. 803–815, paints a picture of the gilded executive mansion down to the Tiffany finishes.

"The President's Wedding," *Harper's Weekly* (June 12, 1886), p. 378, with a description of the flowers at the White House ceremony.

"The White House Conservatories," *Puritan* (July 1900), pp. 449–452, includes a history of the conservatories and photographs of the interiors, including an image of Henry Pfister.

"The White House Conservatories, Washington," *The American Florist* (April 15, 1888), pp. 398–399, describes the mechanical thermometer in the White House greenhouses.

"The White House Gardens," *The American Florist* (August 15, 1889), p. 4, on the garden of old-fashioned flowers behind the greenhouses.

United States Congress. *Annual Reports of the War Department for the Fiscal Year Ended June 30, 1902* (Washington D.C.: Government Printing Office, 1902), p. 2722, with a report on the removal of the plants and demolition of the White House conservatories and greenhouses.

"Washington Floral Fancies," *The New York Times* (January 21, 1894), p. 17, on greenhouse contents and Pfister's professional practices.

"White House Flowers Gone," *The New York Times* (November 10, 1902), p. 7, on Pfister's dismissal.

"White House Posies," *Evening Star* (July 13, 1903), p. 7, describes memories of Alexander McKerichar, George Field, and Henry Pfister of the White House grounds and floral preferences of the presidents and first ladies.

The LuEsther T. Mertz Library at the New York Botanical Garden is a stockpile of treasures for those interested in the history of plants and gardens. Books, rare and curious, are brought out to the joy of the researcher. Its nursery and seed catalogs are available online with full-text search, making it easy to answer questions like "Who sold 'President Cleveland' cannas?" (Answer: Vaughan's Seed Company of Chicago and New York offered them in its 1899 catalog.) Its Lord & Burnham collection includes correspondence regarding greenhouse construction and maintenance from Henry Pfister. Its vertical file on the White House gardens was a small bundle of excellent leads.

In addition to databases and special collections, there are, of course, books:

Bailey, Liberty Hyde. *Annals of Horticulture in North America for the years 1889–1893*, volume 5 (New York: Orange Judd Company, 1894). Pfister's role in the World's Columbian Exposition's Jury in Floriculture is noted on p. 57.

——. *The Standard Cyclopedia of Horticulture in Three Volumes* (New York: The Macmillan Company, 1900). This is the source of the quote "the most highly," related to aquatics, p. 1102, and the information about William Prince's Lombardy poplars, p. 1436, in the earlier chapter "Founders' Grounds."

Baum, L. Frank. *The Annotated Oz*. Ed. Michael Patrick Hearn (New York: W. W. Norton & Company, 2000). Hearn's commentary on the World's Columbian Exposition is on p. 176.

Brinkley, Douglas. *The Wilderness Warrior: Theodore Roosevelt and the Crusade for America* (New York: HarperCollins, 2009).

Bryant, William Cullen, ed. *Picturesque America* (New York: D. Appleton and Company, 1874). A description of the matured Downingesque land-scape of the White House and the Mall is on pp. 455–457.

Earle, Alice Morse. *Old-Time Gardens* (New York: The Macmillan Company, 1901).

Garland, Hamlin. *A Son of the Middle Border* (New York: The Macmillan Company, 1917).

Griswold, Mac, and Eleanor Weller. *The Golden Age of American Gardens: Proud Owners, Private Estates, 1890–1940* (New York: Harry N. Abrams, 2001).

Hill, May Brawley. *Furnishing the Old-Fashioned Garden* (New York: Harry N. Abrams, 1998).

———. *Grandmother's Garden: The Old-Fashioned American Garden: 1865–1915* (New York: Harry N. Abrams, 1995).

Howe, Samuel. *American Country Houses of Today* (New York: Architectural Book Publishing, 1915). The Thomas Hastings quote about the pudding and the sauce is on p. 199.

Johnson, Sophia Orne. *Every Woman Her Own Flower Gardener* (New York: Henry T. Williams, 1874). The quote about vines, "Your homes may," is on p. 62.

Karson, Robin. *A Genius for Place: American Landscapes of the Country Place Era* (Amherst: University of Massachusetts Press, 2007).

Keim, Randolph. *Society in Washington: Its Noted Men, Accomplished Women, Established Customs and Notable Events* (Washington, D.C.: Harrisburg Publishing Company, 1887). This includes information about Pfister's training.

Maloney, Cathy Jean. *World's Fair Gardens: Shaping American Landscapes* (Charlottesville: University of Virginia Press, 2012).

Morris, Sylvia. *Edith Kermit Roosevelt: Portrait of a First Lady* (New York: Random House, 2009). The quote "fine little bad boy," is on p. 316.

Roosevelt, Theodore. *Theodore Roosevelt's Letters to His Children* (New York: Charles Scribner's Sons, 1919). This is the source of letters from Roosevelt to:

- Archie about Quentin's snake adventure, September 21, 1907, p. 200.
- Kermit about Peter Rabbit's funeral, May 28, 1904, pp. 96–97, and the gardens, April 22, 1906, pp. 160–161.
- Quentin about the birds in the White House gardens, June 12, 1904, p. 98.
- Theodore Roosevelt Jr. about the gardens and the tennis, May 28, 1904, pp. 95–96.
- Sarah Schuyler Butler about the macaw, November 3, 1901, pp. 32–33.

Rybczynski, Witold. *A Clearing in the Distance: Frederick Law Olmsted and America in the Nineteenth Century* (New York: Scribner, 1999).

Twain, Mark, and Charles Dudley Warner. *The Gilded Age: A Tale of Today* (Hartford, CT: American Publishing Company, 1873).

Watters, Sam. *Gardens for a Beautiful America, 1895–1935* (New York: Acanthus Press, 2012).

Home Front

As part of the Eleanor Roosevelt Papers Project, George Washington University provides an electronic edition of her "My Day" newspaper column, which she wrote from 1935 through 1962, at http://www.gwu.edu/~erpapers/myday/. The June 9, 1939, column includes "the railings of"; August 31, 1944, includes "managed to keep" and "when the gates."

The Cultural Landscape Foundation maintains a database of its "Pioneers of American Landscape Design" at tclf.org/pioneer. Browse its pages for pictures and biographical and professional information about America's garden makers. You will find the Olmsteds, Beatrix Farrand, and George Burnap at this virtual roundtable of landscape architects and designers.

Despite the wonders of the digital age, many records still exist only on paper. To smooth the way for future garden historians, here are some specifics. The National Archives and Records Administration's Record Group

42 (Entry 97: 31) is the source of the letters from Colonel Spencer Cosby to George H. Brown on May 7, 1909, about the planting for Mrs. Taft's garden party. The file about the East Garden plan (Entry 97: 167) includes Beatrix Jones's plant list and letters from:

- Helen Woodrow Bones to Colonel Cosby, July 8, 1913.
- Beatrix Jones to Colonel Spencer Cosby, July 11, 1913, and August 25, 1913, with planting list and notes.
- Helen Woodrow Bones to Colonel Cosby, September 12, 1913.
- Colonel William H. Harts to Beatrix Jones, October 21, 1913, source of the quote "We shall be."
- Beatrix Farrand to Colonel William H. Harts, January 29, 1916.

The Surveyors' Notebooks for the District of Columbia are a part of the archives of the National Park Service, housed at the National Archives and Records Administration, Record Group 79; working notes for the installation work completed in the East and West gardens in October 1913 are in Box 3, Book 13E. The letter from Frederick Law Olmsted Jr. to Colonel Ulysses S. Grant III, January 24, 1928, is in Record Group 42 (Entry 177: 680).

The National Agricultural Library holds the files on the cherry tree project as part of its U.S. National Arboretum collection. Box 1, Folder 33 includes correspondence from then White House head gardener Charles Henlock about the arrival, inspection, and subsequent burning of the first shipment of trees from Japan.

Aiello, Anthony S. "Japanese Flowering Cherries—A 100-Year-Long Love Affair," *Arnoldia* (April 2012), pp. 2–14.

"Born in Washington, the American Beauty Rose," *The Washington Post* (August 29, 1909), p. 4.

Brenner, Douglas, and Stephen Scanniello. *A Rose by Any Name* (Chapel Hill, NC: Algonquin Books of Chapel Hill, 2009).

Bromley, Michael L. *William Howard Taft and the First Motoring Presidency* (Jefferson, NC: McFarland and Company, 2003). The quote "atmospheric champagne" is on p. 54, cited as "Taft papers, 'Official Functions,' 9/22/1909, p. 164 (reel 599).

"Burpee's Sweet Peas," *The Seed World* (August 4, 1922), p. 31.

Carr, John Foster. "Japanese Garden of Yademos," *American Homes and Gardens* (August 1908), pp. 304–307. The quote "patience and a" is on p. 304.

"Expect White House Dinners To Be Revived," *The New York Times* (March 5, 1921), p. 13.

Fairchild, David. *The World Was My Garden* (New York: Charles Scribner's Sons, 1938). The quote "I found myself" is on p. 413.

"Gardener Enjoys White House Job: William Reeves Recalls Presidents and First Ladies of the Past 32 Years," *The New York Times* (March 14, 1937), p. 17.

"Garden Guardian Quits White House," *The New York Times* (July 12, 1931), p. 9.

Graft, Paula V. "Keeper of the Presidents' Trees," *American Forests* (May 1931), pp. 287–288.

Henlock, Charles, and Margaret Norris. "Flowers for First Ladies," *The Saturday Evening Post* (November 28, 1931), pp. 12–13, 81–83.

"History of the Cherry Trees." National Park Service (www.nps.gov/cherry/cherry-blossom-history.htm) is the source of the letter from Helen Taft to Eliza Scidmore, April 7, 1909.

"'Inside Story' Told of the White House," *The New York Times* (May 9, 1936), p. 17.

Jackson, Kenneth J. *Crabgrass Frontier: The Suburbanization of the United States* (New York: Oxford University Press, 1985).

Jefferson, Roland M., and Alan E. Fusonie. *The Japanese Flowering Cherry Trees of Washington* (Washington, D.C.: USDA, 1977).

"Laddie Boy 'Writes' of White House Life," *The New York Times* (February 8, 1922), p. 5.

Levin, Phyllis Lee. *Edith and Woodrow: The Wilson White House* (New York: Scribner, 2001).

"Michell's Grass Seeds," *The Garden Magazine* (February 1912), p. 53.

O'Toole, Patricia. *When Trumpets Call: Theodore Roosevelt After the White House* (New York: Simon & Schuster, 2005). This includes Roosevelt's comparison of Wilson to Shakespeare's apothecary.

Scidmore, Eliza Ruhamah. *Jinrikisha Days in Japan* (New York: Harper & Brothers, 1891). The quote "A fortnight" is on p. 66.

"She May be Called a Patriot," *The Ladies Home Journal* (October 1921), p. 5. Reports the results of the White House sheep shearing and related auctions.

Stickley, Gustav. "Craftsman Bungalows Built for 'Outdoor' Living," *The Craftsman* (June 1913). The quote "bring the garden" is on p. 330.

Taft, Helen Herron. *Recollections of Full Years* (New York: Dodd, Mead & Company, 1914). The quote "determined, if possible" is on pp. 361–362.

"Taft's Daredevil Chauffeur," *The New York Times Sunday Magazine* (August 15, 1909), p. 4.

"Taft Sworn in Senate Hall," *The New York Times* (March 5, 1909), p. 1.

Tankard, Judith. *Beatrix Farrand: Private Gardens, Public Landscapes* (New York: Monacelli Press, 2009). The quote "to make the" is from an autobiographical statement by Farrand written in 1956, p. 228.

"The White House Gardener: Charles Henlock Has Ruled His Domain in the Reigns of Eight of Our First Ladies," *The New York Times* (March 31, 1929), p. 80.

Wilson, Woodrow, and Edith Bolling Galt. *A President in Love: The Courtship Letters of Woodrow Wilson and Edith Bolling Galt*. Ed. Edwin Tribble (Boston: Houghton Mifflin: 1981). The quote "You are the only" is on p. 30.

Wilson, Woodrow, and Ellen Axson Wilson. *The Priceless Gift: The Love Letters of Woodrow Wilson and Ellen Axson Wilson*. Ed. Eleanor Wilson

McAdoo (New York: McGraw Hill, 1962). Describes Ellen Wilson's immediate intention to redo Roosevelt's Colonial Garden.

"Your Victory Garden." *U.S. Government Campaign to Promote the Production, Sharing, and Proper Use of Food* (Washington, D.C.: Government
Printing Office, 1943).

America the Beautiful

Smithsonian Archives of American Gardens has an abundance of visual
records of the nation's garden history. Many images are available through
the online SIRUS catalog, but one must visit in person to see collections
like the files of Perry Wheeler, the landscape architect who worked with
Bunny Mellon on the East and West Gardens for the Kennedys. The
Wheeler files include correspondence related to furniture, sculpture, and
plants for the gardens, including the pansy order to Blue Mount Nursery. It
also includes correspondence with Henry Hohman.

The Presidential libraries are part of the National Archives and Records
Administration, though each is unique in terms of the type and availability of resources for the researcher.

- The John F. Kennedy Library provides many of its materials online,
  such as the Department of the Interior folder (President's Office Files.
  Departments and Agencies. Interior, 1963: January–June) about the
  costs of the garden projects and the proposal for an in-ground lawn
  irrigation system. The Jacqueline Bouvier Kennedy Onassis Personal
  Papers includes a file on Bunny Mellon and the Rose Garden, which
  includes sketches and correspondence. There is also an oral history
  transcript of an interview with Irvin Williams, available via inter-li-
  brary loan. The library's website (jfklibrary.org) provides an article
  on Jacqueline Kennedy in the White House, including the quotes "that
  dreary Maison Blanche" and "most perfect house."
- The Ronald Reagan Presidential Foundation & Library's website (rea-
  ganfoundation.org) has an excellent article entitled "Second Hand
  Rose."
- The Gerald R. Ford Library, via fordlibrarymuseum.gov, provides the

"Exchange of Toasts between the President and Her Majesty Queen Elizabeth II of the United Kingdom, The Rose Garden, July 7, 1986," digitized from Box 28 of the White House Press Releases.

"Amy Carter Tree House Is Easy, No-Frills Job," *Galveston Daily News* (June 2, 1977), p. 1. This United Press International article has information on both the Kennedy and Carter tree houses.

Bumiller, Elisabeth. "White House Letter; A Pest Looks for, and Gets, Handouts," *The New York Times* (January 13, 2003), p. 13.

Carter, Jimmy. *Christmas in Plains* (New York: Simon & Schuster, 2001).

Conroy, Sarah Booth. "Crabapple Trees Chase Roses Away from the Rose Garden," *Orlando Sentinel* (September 30, 1989), p. G20.

Hilleary, John Thornton. *White House Horticulture* (New York: Vantage Press, 1983).

Jensen, Jens. *Jens Jensen: Writings Inspired by Nature.* Ed. William H. Tishler (Madison: State Historical Society of Wisconsin, 2012). This collection includes the recommendations for a porch in "Improving a Small Country Place," p. 30.

Johnson, Lady Bird. *A White House Diary* (Austin: University of Texas Press, 2007). Johnson's thoughts on beautification are in her entries for March 23, 1964, and June 5, 1967; her ideas for the Children's Garden are from the entry for January 19, 1969.

——. Letter from Lady Bird Johnson to White House Curator James R. Ketchum (undated) is the source of the quote "I think of," related to the Children's Garden. The letter is reprinted in Linda Holden Hoyt's *Presidents' Gardens* (Oxford: Shire Publications, 2013), p. 47.

Langer, Emily. "A Local Life: Everett Hicks, 93, Arborist Who Cared for Mellon Family's Trees," *The Washington Post* (October 8, 2011).

Lewine, Frances. "White House Gardener is Fretful; Whirlybirds Damage His Lawn," *Milwaukee Journal* (June 20, 1958), p. 3.

Knutson, Lawrence L. "White House Gardens Abound in Presidential History," *Indiana Gazette* [Indiana, Pennsylvania] (April 21, 1994), p. 9. This Associated Press article includes Irvin Williams's quote about the apolitical nature of plants.

McCullough, David. *Truman* (New York: Simon & Schuster, 1992). Brick from the White House renovation going to the Mount Vernon gardens is discussed on p. 879.

Mellon, Rachel Lambert. "President Kennedy's Rose Garden," *White House History* (1983), pp. 5–11.

———. "The Jacqueline Kennedy Garden," *House & Garden* (October 1984), pp. 164–169.

Olson, Kay Melchisedech. "Barbara Bush: Why I Garden," *Flower and Garden* (November 1992), pp. 36–39. An interview with First Lady Barbara Bush.

"1,000 Will Get Preview of Renovated White House," *Toledo Blade* (March 23, 1952), p. 6. Source of the quotes about the new azaleas and roses as well as "Needless to say."

Parks, Lillian Rogers, and Frances Spatz Leighton. *My Thirty Years Backstairs at the White House* (New York: Fleet Publishing Company, 1961). This is the source of the story about the gardeners hiding from President Truman, p. 44, and Mamie Eisenhower's "Pink Palace," p. 49.

"President vs. Squirrels and Senator," *The New York Times* (March 23, 1955), p. 1.

"Rebuilt White House Will Be Ready for 3-Day Stay of Juliana in April," *The New York Times* (March 15, 1952), p. 15. Source of the quote "smoothing off a."

Reagan, Ronald. "The Rose Proclaimed the National Floral Emblem of the United States of America." Statute 101, Proclamation 5574 (Washington D.C.: Government Printing Office, 1986).

Reginato, James. "Bunny Mellon's Secret Garden," *Vanity Fair* (August 2010), pp. 150–169.

Strumpf, Manny E., and Candace Garry. "Whitey's Role At the White House." *Courier: The National Park Service Newsletter* (August 1980), pp. 12–13.

Thayer, Mary Van Rensselaer. *Jacqueline Kennedy: The White House Years* (Boston: Little, Brown, 1971). Includes Jacqueline Kennedy's quote about the White House lawn driving the president crazy on p. 143.

Thurman, James N. "A Gardener's View of Life at 1600 Pennsylvania Avenue," *Christian Science Monitor* (April 13, 1998), p. 1. With descriptions of squirrels and peanuts and raccoons and goldfish.

"Truman Decides to Have a Porch At White House to Cost $15,000," *The New York Times* (January 3, 1948), p. 15.

Truman, Harry S. *Dear Bess: The Letters from Harry to Bess Truman 1910–1959*. Ed. Robert H. Ferrell (New York: W. W. Norton & Company, 1983). HST's letter to Bess Truman, September 12, 1946, is the source of "the great white jail."

Truman, Margaret. *First Ladies: An Intimate Group Portrait of White House Wives* (New York: Random House, 1995). This includes the quote from her mother on "First Ladying."

Weisinger, Mort. "First Florist of the Land," *The Saturday Evening Post* (September 10, 1949), p. 17.

Whitcomb, John, and Claire Whitcomb. *Real Life at the White House: Two Hundred Years of Daily Life at America's Most Famous Residence* (New York: Routledge, 2000). To read about the spray painting of brown patches on the lawn, see p. 355.

Is Green the New Red, White, and Blue?

Allen, Will, and Fritz Haeg. *Edible Estates: Attack on the Front Lawn* (New York: Metropolis Books, 2010).

Benac, Nancy. "Time to Green This Old (White) House—Again," *Christian Science Monitor* (March 30, 2009), p. 15.

Bumiller, Elisabeth. "Through 7 Presidents, Thousands of Bulbs and a Few Dogs, the Keeper of the Trowel," *The New York Times* (April 25, 2005), p. 18.

Bush, Laura. *Spoken From the Heart* (New York, Simon & Schuster, 2010). The quote "That season" is from p. 243.

——. "Mrs. Bush's Remarks at Press Preview of White House Spring Garden Tour" (April 16, 2004). Accessed via georgewbush-whitehouse. archives.gov.

Choukas-Bradley, Melanie. "Historic Trees & Gardens of 1600 Pennsylvania Avenue." *American Forests* (Summer 2010), pp. 36–45. For those interested in the nation's capital and its tree plantings overall, see this author's *City of Trees: The Complete Field Guide to the Trees of Washington, D.C.* (Charlottesville: University of Virginia Press, 2008).

Clinton, Hillary Rodham. *An Invitation to the White House: At Home with History* (New York: Simon & Schuster, 2000). The quote "I often find myself" is from p. 118.

——. "Interview of the President and the First Lady by National Geographic" (July 25, 1995). This is an internal transcript from the White House Office of the Press Secretary that discusses the vegetables grown on the roof garden during the Clinton administration. It is available via clintonlibrary.gov.

Dickens, Charles. *American Notes* (New York: John W. Lovell Company, 1883). The description of Washington is on p. 695.

Finn, David. *20th Century American Sculpture in the White House Garden* (New York: Harry N. Abrams, 2001).

Hatch, Peter. "Jefferson Plants in White House Kitchen Garden," *Monticello* (Spring 2001), p. 1.

Kotz, Mary Lynn. "At the White House: The First Lady's Sculpture Garden," *Sculpture* (July/August 1998), pp. 22–29, accessed via sculpture.org. This is the source of the quote "When I moved."

Michael Van Valkenburgh Associates. "Pennsylvania Avenue Washington D.C. (2002–2005)." Accessed via mvvainc.com.

Obama, Michelle. *American Grown: The Story of the White House Kitchen Garden* (New York: Crown Publishing, 2012).

———. "First Lady Michelle Obama's Remarks on the Cherry Blossom Festival Centennial," Office of the First Lady (March 27, 2012). Accessed via whitehouse.gov/blog.

Pollan, Michael. "Abolish the White House Lawn," Op-ed, *The New York Times* (May 5, 1991), pp. 4, 17.

———. *The Botany of Desire* (New York: Random House, 2001).

Shear, Michael D., and Jim Yardley. "An Exchange of Views, Some in Accord," *The New York Times* (March 28, 2014), A10, on the visit of President Obama to Pope Francis.

Tallamy, Douglas W. *Bringing Nature Home* (Portland, OR: Timber Press, 2007).

Tortorello, Michael. "Plants with Roots Attached," *The New York Times* (July 10, 2014), D1.

Waters, Alice. *Edible Schoolyard* (San Francisco: Chronicle Books, 2001).

First Gardeners

In addition to sources cited earlier, ancestry.com was a valuable resource for researching life events, family relationships, and city directories. Other sources included:

Thomas Magraw

Letter from Anthony Charles Casenove to James Madison, December 13, 1811. Accessed via Founders Online.

Charles Bizet

Allgor, Catherine, ed. *The Queen of America: Mary Cutts's Life of Dolley Madison* (Charlottesville: University of Virginia Press, 2012).

Taylor, Elizabeth Downing. *A Slave in the White House: Paul Jennings and the Madisons* (New York: Macmillan, 2012). The quotes from the Cutts memoir are on page 85.

Letters accessed via Founders Online from:
- James Madison to James Monroe, July 16, 1810.
- James Monroe to James Madison, July 25, 1810.
- Thomas Jefferson to James Madison, March 10, 1817.
- James Madison to Thomas Jefferson, April 10, 1817.
- James Madison to Richard Cutts, October 12, 1817.

John Ousley

Naturalization papers from the Circuit Court, District of Columbia dated May 23, 1825.

Speech of Hon. Levi Woodbury on Mr. Clay's Resolutions (Boston: Printed at No. 1 Devonshire Street, 1840), p. 4 provided Ousley's appointment date and salary.

John Watt

Census and tax records accessed via ancestry.com.

George McLeod

The previously cited "Gardening at the White House" provided the reference to George McLeod's tenure there.

"Prince George's County Historic Site Summary Sheet for McLeod-Forrester House," dated 1974.

Alexander McKerichar

The previously cited "White House Posies" included the story of President Grant's celebratory drink with "Mac."

"Alexander McKerichar" (obituary) *Florists' Review* (August 6, 1914), p. 20.

"Guarded Their Sleep; To Sleep Among Them," *The Washington Herald* (July 28, 1914) p. 2.

George Field
"The Bridal Bouquet," *The Washington Post* (February 18, 1906), p. 6.

"Vesey Buys $15,000 Worth of Orchids," *The Fort Wayne Daily News* (July 7, 1916), p. 14.

"Washington D.C. Various Notes," *Florists' Review* (July 20, 1916), p. 32.

Henry Pfister
Letter from Henry Pfister to Frederick Coville, August 13, 1896, and January 30, 1899, in the collection of the National Archives, College Park, Maryland.

Nehrling, Henry. *My Garden in Florida* (Estero, Florida: The American Eagle, 1944). Henry Pfister is mentioned sending plants to Dr. Nehrling on p. 601.

"Notes," *Garden and Forest* (March 24, 1897), p. 120.

Passport application dated February 5, 1915, accessed via ancestry.com.

"White House Gardener," *Lockport Journal* (October 24, 1901), p. 1.

George Hay Brown
Brown, George H. "Notes on Public Playgrounds," Appendix B of Report of the Chief of Engineers, U. S. Army (Washington D.C.: U.S. Government Printing Office, 1903), pp. 2666–2669.

_____. "The City Parks and Park Places of Washington, D.C.," Appendix B of Report of the Chief of Engineers, U. S. Army (Washington D.C.: U.S. Government Printing Office, 1903), pp. 2238–2239.

"George Hay Brown" (obituary), *The Washington Post* (November 24, 1909), p. 3.

Untitled obituary, *The National Tribune* (December 9, 1909), p. 5.

Charles Henlock

The previously cited *The Japanese Flowering Cherry Trees of Washington* includes a biographical summary of Henlock.

William Saunders Reeves

Gardner, Charles Milo. *The Grange, Friend of the Farmer* (Washington D.C.: The National Grange, 1949). Includes information about William Saunders, the Grange, and the navel orange.

"President Wilson's Flock," *The Illinois Agriculturist* (April 1919), p. 84.

Roosevelt, Eleanor. *The Autobiography of Eleanor Roosevelt* (Boston: Da Capo Press, 1992). The quote "His reticence" is on p. 73.

Robert M. Redmond

"Keeping House at the White House," *The New York Times* (December 28, 1952), pp. 7–8.

"New Setting for New White House," *The New York Times* (June 22, 1952), p. 188.

"Spring is Time for Gardening at White House," *Brownwood (Texas) Bulletin* (March 22, 1954), p. 1.

"White House Posies Earn Their Own Keep Today," *The Ogden (Utah) Standard-Examiner* (June 7, 1953), p. 2.

Irvin Williams

Axler, Judith. "At the White House He Gardens (and at Home, Too)," *The New York Times* (October 12, 1968), p. 28.

Knutson, Lawrence L. "Andrew Jackson's Tree Grows into a New Millennium." *Ludington (Michigan) Daily News* (May 18, 1999), p. 3.

Dale Haney

"Dale Haney White House Grounds Superintendent," a biographical summary from georgewbush-whitehouse.archives.gov.

Superville, Darlene. "Dale Haney: White House Groundskeeper" and "Bo's Best Friend," *Huff Post Green* (March 18, 2010) accessed via huffingtonpost.com.

Acknowledgments

To JENNY BENT, an agent and a marvel, as well as my niece.

To Tom Fischer, best editor ever, I hope someday to meet you face to face, and to Mollie Firestone for the splendid encore.

To Thelma Achenbach, Devin and Judy Bent, Susan Castellan, Jane Davenport, Cindy Dickinson, Linda O'Gorman, Gail Reuben, Joan Ryder, Sandra Swan, and Pamela Zave, whose careful reading inspired many improvements.

To Cathy Messmer and Sarah Hartman who prospected and found gold.

To Doris Crater and Alice Wade, always on the lookout for interesting tidbits.

To Yolanda Fundora whose able eye and artistic prowess made the illustrations sing.

To W. Barry Thomson, for answers.

To the Honorable Rodney Frelinghuysen and his staff, especially Steve Silvestri, who persisted.

To Jim Adams, National Park Service Supervisory Horticulturist for the White House, huge thanks for the plant inventory, the thorough tour, and all-round responsiveness. With you and your team of the "Green and Gray," the country's First Garden is in good hands.

To the librarians, for whom a private place in paradise is surely reserved, especially: Laura Barry at the Historical Society of Washington D.C.'s

Kiplinger Library; Anna Clutterbuck-Cook at the Massachusetts Historical Society; Kelly Crawford at the Smithsonian Archives of American Gardens; Janet Evans at the Pennsylvania Horticultural Society's McLean Library; Susan Fraser, Stephen Sinon, Marie Long, and Mia D'Avanza at The New York Botanical Garden's LuEsther Mertz Library; Robert Schriek at the Library of the Chathams; Leora Siegel at the Chicago Botanic Garden's Lenhardt Library; Lynn Stanko at the National Agricultural Library; Ines Zalduendo at the Harvard Graduate School of Design; and the librarians, archivists, and media specialists at the Library of Congress and the National Archives and Records Administration, including the presidential libraries.

To the subscribers of ancestry.com, especially Robin Wierzbicki for material on Andrew McKerichar and Katherine Mendenhall on John Ousley.

To Edie Loening and Susan Van Tassel, for the gems from The Garden Club of America.

To Seamus Maclennan, for viable seed that grew into this book.

And to Kirke Bent, who still makes history come alive.

Illustration Sources
and Credits

Pages 2, 12 top, 12 bottom left, 12 bottom right, 25, 26, 36, 49 top, 50, 51, 52, 53, 65, 67 top, 80 bottom, 81, 94, 97, 98, 108 bottom, 109 bottom, 112, 114, 115 bottom, 118, 124, 125, 127, 128, 131, 132 bottom, 138, 139 bottom, 142, 143, 144, 148, 149, 152, 160 top, 161, 165, 168, 172, 181, 182, 183 left, 184 top and bottom left, 186, 187 left, 188, 191 bottom, 192, 193, 202 right, 208, 224, 226, 232, 239, 241, endpapers: Courtesy of the Library of Congress

Page 4: Courtesy of the Smithsonian Institution Libraries, Washington D.C.

Pages 10, 30, 46, 59, 80 top, 154, 167, 190, 205 bottom left, 261: The LuEsther T. Mertz Library of The New York Botanical Garden

Pages 18, 42, 54, 83: Courtesy National Gallery of Art, Washington D.C.

Page 21 left: Courtesy of Mount Vernon Ladies' Association

Page 23 top: Gilcrease Museum

Page 23 bottom: © The Metropolitan Museum of Art. Image Source: Art Resource, NY

Pages 32, 49 bottom: Free Library of Philadelphia, Print and Picture Collection

Page 39: Courtesy Department of Special Collections, Stanford University Libraries

Page 44: Courtesy Thomas Jefferson Foundation, Inc.

Pages 47, 177: The McLean Library, Pennsylvania Horticultural Society

Page 63: Published courtesy of the Fruitlands Museums, Harvard, MA

Pages 67 bottom, 90, 107, 108 top, 109 top, 130, 147, 171, 262: National Archives and Records Administration

Pages 69, 70: Reproduced by permission of The Huntington Library, San Marino, CA

Pages 72, 202 left: White House Historical Association (White House Collection)

Page 74: Collection of the Massachusetts Historical Society

Page 77 right: From the Rare Book Collection of the Lenhardt Library of the Chicago Botanic Garden

Page 79: Smithsonian American Art Museum, Washington D.C./Art Resource, NY

Pages 88, 96, 156–157: The Historical Society of Washington D.C.

Pages 92, 263: White House Historical Association

Pages 133, 211 top, 213: Smithsonian Institution, Archives of American Gardens

Page 146: Clarke Family Papers Collection, Special Collections, Florida Atlantic University Libraries

Page 170: The Woodrow Wilson Presidential Library and Museum at his Birthplace, Staunton, VA

Pages 174–175, 178–179: Beatrix Jones Farrand Collection, 1866–1959, Environmental Design Archives, University of California, Berkeley

Page 180: The President Woodrow Wilson House, a Site of the National Trust for Historic Preservation, Washington D.C.

Pages 194, 205 top: AP Photo/HWG

Page 195: © Disney

Page 200: © Corbis

Page 201: National Park Service

Page 203: Special Collections, National Agricultural Library

All other images are from the author's collection.

Index

For my parents, Mary and Joseph "Mac" McDowell

Published in 2016 by Timber Press, Inc.
The Haseltine Building
133 S.W. Second Avenue, Suite 450
Portland, Oregon 97204-3527

timberpress.com

Printed in China
Text design by Patrick Barber
Jacket design by Anna Eshelman

Library of Congress Cataloging-in-Publication Data

Names: McDowell, Marta.
Title: All the presidents' gardens: Madison's cabbages to Kennedy's roses: how the White
   House grounds have grown with America / by Marta McDowell.
Description: Portland, Oregon: Timber Press, Inc., 2016. | Includes bibliographical
   references and index.
Identifiers: LCCN 2015029811 | ISBN 9781604695892
Subjects: LCSH: White House Gardens (Washington, D.C.)—History. | Gardens—
   Washington (D.C.)—History. | Horticulture—Washington (D.C.)—History.
Classification: LCC SB453.2.W35 M33 2016 | DDC 635.09753—dc23 LC record available at
   http://lccn.loc.gov/2015029811

A catalog record for this book is also available from the British Library.